THE ART OF PROTEST

JO RIPPON

First published in 2019 by
Palazzo Editions Ltd
15 Church Road
London, SW13 9HE
United Kingdom
www.palazzoeditions.com

Design and layout © 2019 Palazzo Editions Ltd
Text © 2019 by Jo Rippon

All rights reserved. No part of this publication may be reproduced in any form or by any means – electronic, mechanical, photocopying, recording, or otherwise – or stored in any retrieval system of any nature without prior written permission from the copyright holders.
The moral right of the author has been asserted in accordance with the Copyright Designs and Patents Act 1988.

A CIP catalogue record for this book is available from the British Library.

ISBN: 978-1-78675-027-3

10 9 8 7 6 5 4 3 2 1

Colour reproduction by Imagewrite Ltd
Printed and bound in China by C&C Offset Printing
Designed by Becky Clarke for Palazzo Editions

CONTENTS

9 — FOREWORD BY ANISH KAPOOR

13 — NO HUMAN BEING IS ILLEGAL . . .

35 — WOMEN ARE LIKE TEABAGS . . .

57 — IF A BULLET SHOULD ENTER MY BRAIN . . .

79 — THOSE WHO LOVE PEACE . . .

103 — UNTHINKING RESPECT FOR AUTHORITY . . .

125 — HATE IS TOO GREAT A BURDEN . . .

147 — WE ARE USING RESOURCES . . .

171 — AFTERWORD BY AMNESTY INTERNATIONAL

174 SOURCES • 176 ACKNOWLEDGMENTS

ARTISTS ARE HERE TO DISTURB THE PEACE.

James Baldwin
AUTHOR AND ACTIVIST

FOREWORD

BY ANISH KAPOOR

One Movement, One Message, Many Voices.
Seymour Chwast for Amnesty International
1988, USA

Featuring a drawing from American graphic designer Seymour Chwast, this poster was produced for the Human Rights Now! campaign in 1988. Human Rights Now! was a worldwide campaign to increase awareness of Amnesty International and to commemorate the fortieth anniversary of the Universal Declaration of Human Rights.

To make art I need to have the freedom of an inner life, freedom to think, to feel, to disobey, to refuse. Freedom to participate and, most importantly, freedom to withhold my participation.

The art object is of course only partially given place and meaning by the artist. The circle of its power is completed by the viewer. Art does not dictate, it invites participation and in so doing it is a bridge to meaning made by the life experience and sensibility of the viewer. The art object is therefore not a closed singularity. It exists as a communal act of participation. This is a process that depends on the freedom of others as well as that of my own. The art object is by its very nature therefore a deeply political act of affirmation and participation.

These fundamental freedoms of being cannot, sadly, be taken for granted. They are fragile and vulnerable. Governments all over the world control the limits of "freedom." In these difficult times we find ourselves at the limits of citizen activism and unable to trust official routes to information and therefore to power. The structures of capitalism have built an edifice of control from which it is impossible for the citizen to wrestle free, increasingly through the complete control of all access to food, clothing, housing, and all the other necessities of life. It is hard to imagine today a system that can replace capitalism and yet we must. The splitting off of what can be made "other": Workers, Women, Tribal groups, Blacks, Asians, Refugees, LGBTQ's, the Disabled etc. These are the unwanted and are anathema. They are the outsiders, but to paraphrase Marx and Engels: *if one is in chains we are all in chains*. This process dehumanizes us all. It tramples who we are. It crushes our human potential and the potential of humanity.

UNITE

Protest is our way to assert our freedom of association—*the one for the many and the many for the one*. We inhabit a zeitgeist which we cannot separate ourselves from. Art does not happen in a state of isolation, it is the here and now and the here and now has urgency.

The political slogan, the poster, and the sign or symbol of a movement or group are images around which we are called to unite. They speak the voice of an individual but capture the voice of the many and on occasion even the voice of a generation. These images matter, they are the signs of the unrest in our souls, they tell us of our will to freedom and of our unwillingness to conform. The right image has an uncanny ability to voice my individual pain, for in truth injustice is mine alone . . . I must suffer it alone . . . even if I am able to find comrades who suffer as I do.

Goya's *The Disasters of War* gives face to the innocents in the firing line waiting to die. Tragically caught in the terror of some inevitable but manmade disaster. Picasso finds in his *Guernica* a completely new language for the cry of innocents

Prisoner of Conscience
Joop Lieverst for
Amnesty International
1969, Netherlands

A prisoner of conscience marks off the days in his cell. In its early years, Amnesty International focused on Articles 18 and 19 of the UN Declaration of Human Rights, which deal with freedom of thought and expression.

as they are bombed into submission. Today's contemporary artists continue to articulate and protest injustice; the activist group Pussy Riot has made performance an act of political disobedience. Cuban artist Tania Bruguera is to be admired for her stand against state control. Petr Pavlensky, Ai Weiwei, and many other colleagues find political voice in response to the oppressive forces that govern us. The images in this book are a compendium of the will to a voice. They are a first step to self-determination and dignity. Collectively they declare a refusal to be looked at or judged from the outside. A refusal to limit the diversity that is self-determination. A refusal to be drawn in to the commonality of means that reduces all peoples and all causes to the simplified language of the majority.

The poster, the banner, and the slogan have a homemade immediacy that is a sign of quotidian consciousness. Their mostly simple means help to ensure availability both as artifact and as message. We are all poster-makers, and through them we all attest to the unrest in our souls and our will to dignity.

NO HUMAN BEING IS ILLEGAL. THAT IS A CONTRADICTION IN TERMS. HOW CAN A HUMAN BEING BE ILLEGAL?

Elie Wiesel

NOBEL LAUREATE AND HOLOCAUST SURVIVOR

Share
Alfred F. Burke for the Jewish Relief Campaign
1917, USA

The First World War decimated much of Europe, displacing large numbers of citizens, with European Jews among the hardest hit. Although they had fought on both sides, they were persecuted by both Russia and Germany for enemy collaboration. Cast as untrustworthy criminals, it was left to overseas Jewish communities, such as the Jewish Relief Campaign, to provide aid. Here, a colossal Columbia, goddess-like and wearing the cap of liberty, manifests almost dreamlike as she proffers the bounty of America to a huddled group of haggard refugees. Depicted in dark colors and appearing destitute, the group, one of whom reaches up towards the plentiful tray, present a stark contrast to the luminous colors of the poster's radiant backdrop. To the right, the skyline of New York throws up the silhouette of the Statue of Liberty, which from around 1920 usurped Columbia as the nation's favored epitome of freedom, perhaps due in part to the heavy publicizing of Liberty war bonds during the First World War.

War Rages in France
Harry Everett Townsend
for the United States Food Administration
c. 1917, USA

This poster shows refugees in a ruined city. It was illustrated by American artist Harry Everett Townsend, who had been living in France working as an illustrator until the outbreak of the First World War brought him home to America. He first designed posters for relief efforts, such as this one published by the United States Food Administration (USFA), before being recruited as an official war artist in 1918. Food had become a weapon in the First World War and America, being the largest producer, responded by setting up the USFA—overseen by Herbert Hoover—to aid fleeing European refugees and front-line soldiers. Its main remit was food conservation. At the time, posters relied on the power of illustration to capture the plight of the human and present a persuasive image that pulled at the heartstrings of America, such as the print here portraying mainly women and children. Posters also needed to inspire people to act voluntarily, a tactic that Hoover favored over enforced and regulated rationing. The USFA operated until the war ended, and although it was largely successful, the end of the war did not spell the end of food shortages. Many refugees still faced starvation, and a successor agency—the American Relief Administration (ARA)—was formed in February 1919, again headed by Hoover.

THE ART OF PROTEST

> "What more can these immigrants from Italy expect? It is not every prisoner who has a President of Harvard University throw on the switch for him."
>
> -- Heywood Broun in N. Y. World

"A NATION RINGED BY WALLS WILL ONLY IMPRISON ITSELF."
Barack Obama
FIRST AFRICAN AMERICAN US PRESIDENT

Lest We Perish
Ethel Franklin Betts for the American Committee for Relief in the Near East (ACRNE)
1918, USA

A young Armenian girl painted by American illustrator Ethel Franklin Betts fronts this campaign to raise money for refugees from the Armenian genocide during the early twentieth century. With outstretched arms imploring the viewer, this poster published by the American Committee for Relief in the Near East (ACRNE)—today the Near East Foundation— was one of the committee's most iconic. It was also notable for the way in which it helped prime America for its longstanding practice of philanthropy. What started as a grassroots campaign founded in 1915 in response to reports of atrocities against Ottoman Armenians inspired American citizens to raise over $116 million—the largest humanitarian effort in America thus far—and in 1919 saw ACRNE recognized with a congressional charter. From 1915 to 1930, the committee helped save the lives of over a million refugees.

Untitled
Sacco-Vanzetti Defense Committee
1927, USA

This broadside was published just after the execution by electric chair of two Italian-born Americans, Nicola Sacco, a thirty-two-year-old shoemaker, and Bartolomeo Vanzetti, a twenty-nine-year-old fish peddler. Seven years earlier they had been charged with the murders of a watchman and a paymaster during an armed heist at a shoe factory in Boston, Massachusetts. The evidence against them was insubstantial, and many Americans believed their immigrant background predestined their prosecution, as did their political beliefs. Both Sacco and Vanzetti were ardent anticapitalists and members of an anarchist movement. This did not bode well in 1920s America, which, in the wake of the 1917 Russian Revolution, was living through its first "Red Scare" and the fear that anarchists and aliens were plotting an uprising in the United States. The text of the poster is taken from an article written in defense of Sacco and Vanzetti by journalist Heywood Broun on August 5, 1927, in the *New York World*. The Harvard president alluded to is Abbott Lowell, who had been part of a three-man advisory board appointed by Judge Webster Thayer to assess the fairness of the trial and who subsequently rejected appeals for clemency.

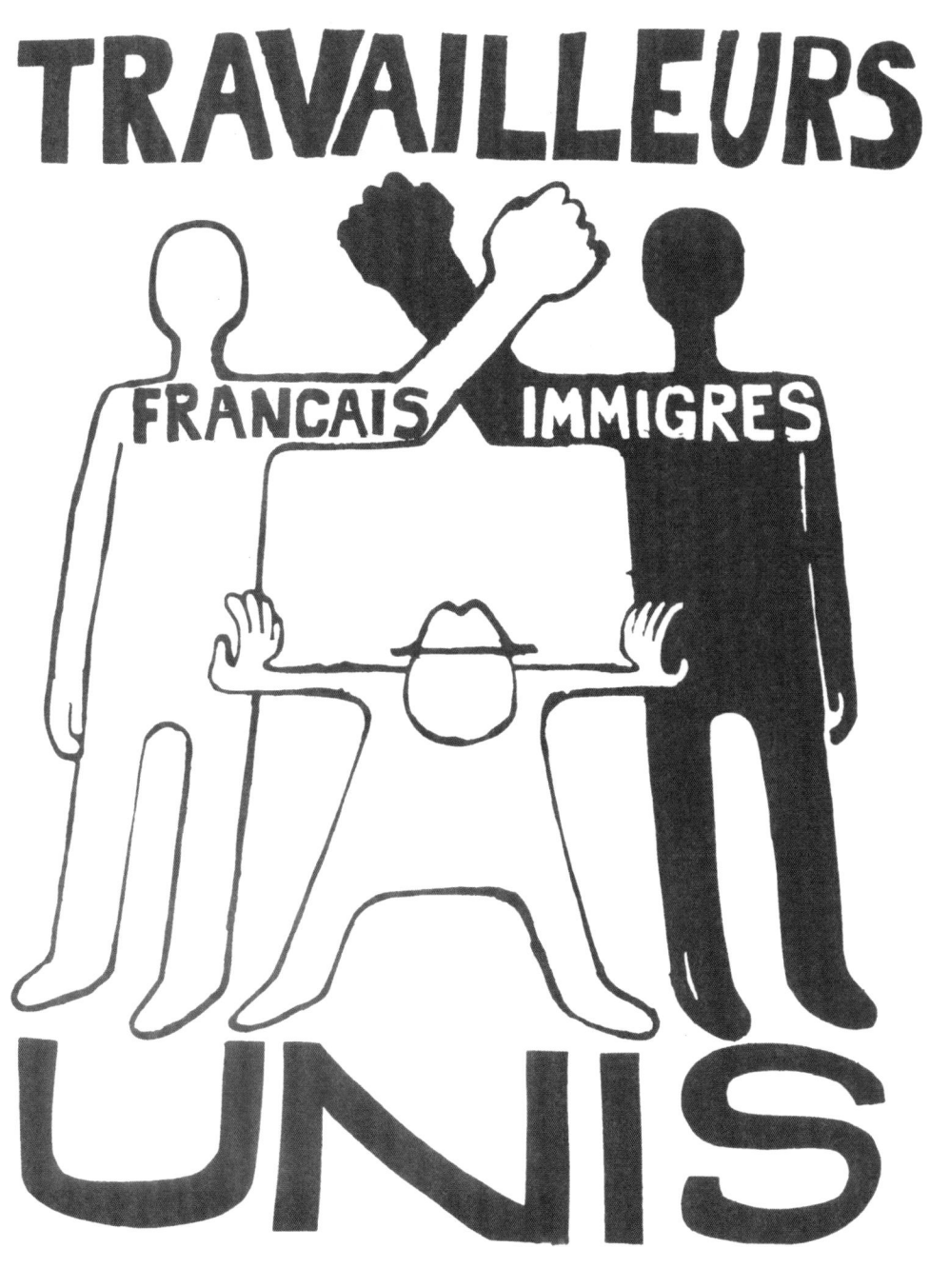

Cego? Mudo? Não!
Artist unknown
c.1970, France

This poster highlights the prejudice that Portuguese immigrant workers faced in France during the 1960s and 1970s, decades that saw the largest ever influx of Portuguese people to France, with shanty towns appearing suddenly on the outskirts of Paris. Many came to escape poverty—France being industrially more advanced and desperate for cheap labor—but some also came as political refugees escaping the dictatorship of António de Oliveira Salazar, or to avoid conscription to wars in Portugal's African colonies. Most came directly from rural villages and within the context of metropolitan Paris were often viewed as unsophisticated and a bit backward. Add to this the Pide (Salazar's secret police), who infiltrated French factories to spy on the immigrant workers because of fears that communist tendencies might be exported back to Portugal, and many Portuguese in France faced oppression and exploitation from all sides and were vulnerable to discrimination. This hand-drawn poster shows a sketch of a man wearing sunglasses and with his mouth covered. It is accompanied by the questions "Cego? Mudo?" ("Blind? Mute?") and answered with a firm "Não!" (No!") highlighted in red. The last word of the poster, "Analfabeto" ("Illiterate"), offers further explanation and an implied defense of the Portuguese workers.

Travailleurs Unis
Atelier Populaire
1968, France

Workers united is the theme of this poster, and its interconnected design captures the central role of immigration in questions of social justice. On the left is a white figure with the word "Francais" tattooed across his front, while his opposite is printed solid black with the word "Immigres." Their right arms are held aloft and crossed in solidarity, their fists enlarged to show strength and resistance. A smaller figure between the Frenchman and the immigrant worker wears a hat indicating authority and is pushing them apart with his hands. The poster was printed by Atelier Populaire during the student revolt of May 1968. Nanterre University—from where the protests emerged—was situated next to slum housing, and its students bore daily witness to the social injustices faced by immigrants. Recruitment of immigrants to the students' protest was seen as crucial not just for their own emancipation, but for the strength they added to the common cause; immigrant workers embodied the imperialistic oppression that students were protesting—cheap labor being central to capitalism as well as a means to undermine the political strength of the working class.

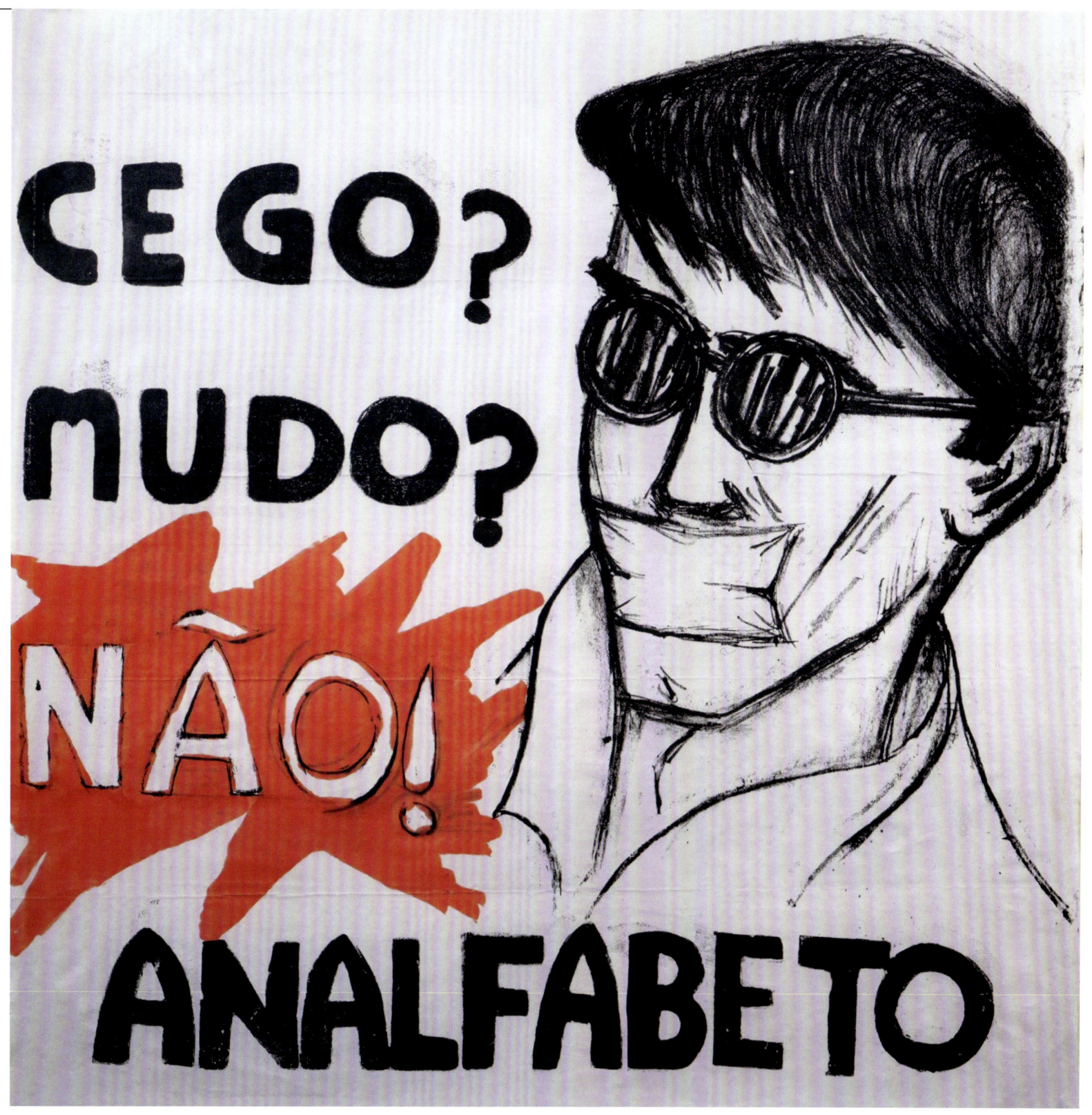

"THE WAY A GOVERNMENT TREATS REFUGEES IS VERY INSTRUCTIVE, BECAUSE IT SHOWS YOU HOW THEY WOULD TREAT THE REST OF US IF THEY THOUGHT THEY COULD GET AWAY WITH IT."
Tony Benn
BRITISH POLITICIAN AND WRITER

What's The Difference?
United Nations High Commissioner for Refugees (UNHCR)
1994–1997, Worldwide

In 1993, the UNHCR approached the LEGO Group for permission to use the LEGO® minifigure in their refugee awareness work. The LEGO Group gave permission, and a campaign of advertisements and posters starring the LEGO minifigure was created. "What's The Difference?" was one of four posters produced, all of which were reissued in 1998 for the fiftieth anniversary of the Universal Declaration of Human Rights. Of the twelve identical LEGO minifigures, the first nine are branded with derogatory descriptions such as "scum," "foreign trash," and "vermin." The last three are labeled "refugee," "you," and "me." Together with the homogeneity of the figures the words expose social prejudice, discriminatory language, and misconceptions about refugees, as well as the power of language in forming opinions. The UNHCR was created In 1950 to help the millions of Europeans displaced during the Second World War, with a timeline of three years. Seventy years later, and with 68.5 million refugees worldwide—the highest ever levels of displacement on record—the UNHCR is still operational.

De la tierra somos ¡no somos ilegales!
Carlos A. Cortéz
1984, USA

From Mexican-American printmaker, poet, and lifelong political activist Carlos A. Cortéz, this image was produced in support of immigrant workers in the United States. Bold-cut letters at the top and bottom declare: "We are of the earth. We are not illegal." Sandwiched between, a black and white image focuses on a man, woman, and child. The man wears a sombrero, which indicates Mexican heritage and, as it shelters both the woman and child, suggests that they are a family. The strong-cut lines on their faces add depth aesthetically and symbolically. In the background is a representation of the Pyramid of the Sun, the largest structure of the ancient Mexican city Teotihuacan. To the left is a corn stalk, an important crop to Native Americans, who taught European settlers how to cultivate it. The son of immigrants to the US, Cortéz felt a strong bond with people experiencing discrimination and used his art to promote social change. This carefully composed graphic work was designed to counter the belief that these people are "illegal aliens" by reminding us of their long-standing connection to the land, which extends beyond the event of European colonization.

PARASITE	**CRIMINAL**	**FOREIGN TRASH**	**PIG**
TROUBLEMAKER	**FREELOADER**	**VERMIN**	**SLACKER**
SCUM	**REFUGEE**	**YOU**	**ME**

WHAT'S THE DIFFERENCE?

Nasty names. Shocking even in print. But all too common if you're unlucky enough to be a refugee.

Wait. Why are "you" and "me" among them? And why is every figure identical? They're all the same!

Exactly!

You see, refugees *are* just like you and me. So what's the difference?

There's really only one: fear.

While our homes are safe and our rights are protected, their homes have been left behind and the rights they once enjoyed were swept away by violence and hatred. They've been living in constant fear for their lives.

UNHCR

United Nations High Commissioner for Refugees

That's why they've had to leave their country. That's why they are refugees. Of course they wish they were back home – wouldn't you? But it's still too dangerous, and for now we must continue to offer them our help.

So please, don't get mad at refugees.

Instead, save your breath for the situation that's *made* them refugees.

الملاذ!
أوروبا
البوسنة والهرسك

سليم أورنانوفتش:

تُرى من الذي يقيم في منزلي؟
محنة اللاجئين والمشردين

منظمة العفو الدولية

"Who's living in my house?"
Amnesty International
1997, Worldwide

With the focus around an image taken by photojournalist Howard Davies in 1996, this poster presents the reality of returning to a home country previously ravaged by war. The subject of the photo is a Bosnian Muslim refugee returning to his former home after four years of living in the UK. However, this homecoming image is not one of jubilance but rather, rendered in stark black and white, one of loss. Standing alone, the man, with few belongings, looks at something out of frame. It has been raining and you can see his reflection in the wet road. Behind him is a house under construction. The text reads "The sanctuary of Europe. Bosnia and Herzegovina. Who's living in my house? The plight of refugees and displaced persons." The poster was produced to coincide with the publication of Amnesty International's 1997 report *Bosnia-Herzegovina: "Who's living in my house?" Obstacles to the safe return of refugees and displaced people*. The obstacles covered in the report included having no homes to return to due to them being destroyed, planted with mines, or occupied by others.

U.S. Trade and Immigration Policy
Ricardo Levins Morales
2007, USA

This intricate print perfectly captures the United States' relationship with Latin America. Without the need for words, it articulates how migrants from Central America are trapped in a tyrannical cycle, between a US foreign policy that forces them to flee and a domestic policy that favors detention, deportation or, at best, cheap labor. A long history of intervention, either through US-bankrolled military coups, exploitation of natural resources, or corporate pillage, is inextricable from the displacement of people from Central America. Here, the central figure—US capitalism personified, dressed in a shirt patterned with dollar signs—sets the land to the right alight. The inhabitants flee, facing an arduous river crossing before being scooped up by the figure; the "lucky" ones are forced to work under the smoke-filled sky, while others are thrown in an overcrowded jail. Just below the figure's fire-lighting arm, there is a bridge over the river, across which trucks loaded with goods travel unimpeded to the other side.

Human Dignity, Human Rights
Photograph by Steve McCurry and design by Pentagram for Amnesty International USA for the Demand Dignity campaign
2010, USA

The girl in this poster is an Afghan refugee whose picture was taken in 2002 by American photographer Steve McCurry. It uses the same close-up headshot style of "Afghan Girl"—an earlier photo which McCurry is perhaps best known for, of another Afghan refugee that he took in 1984 and was featured on the cover of *National Geographic*. As in that photograph, the girl here looks directly at the viewer. The image has been overlaid with a semiopaque stencil of letters that spell: "Human Dignity, Human Rights." Below we learn that "this ten-year-old Afghan refugee lives in Peshawar, Pakistan, and has never seen her homeland." Most Afghans in Pakistan are refugees who have fled wars in their homeland. Since the Soviet invasion in 1979, 2.7 million refugees have crossed the border to neighboring Pakistan. Many of those under thirty years of age have been born in Pakistan, although they are still considered Afghan citizens. In 2018, Pakistan's prime minister, Imran Khan, promised to grant passports to refugees whose children had been born in Pakistan. He later faced a backlash from the country's military.

Untitled
Chadi Marouf for Solidarity for Palestinian Human Rights
2015, Canada

The poster calls for a "Manif Nocturne" or night demonstration to commemorate "La Nakba" (literally, *disaster*)—the Arabic name given to the events of the 1948 Palestinian exodus, when more than 700,000 Palestinian Arabs fled or were expelled from their homes to make way for the Israeli declaration of independence. It is considered by many as the start of Palestinian struggles, and the status of these refugees is a key issue in the ongoing conflict. The poster's illustration fuses two individual posters from 1984 by Palestinian artist Abdel Rahman Al Muzain—*Land Day*, which shows a peasant farmer holding a pickaxe in a symbolic, determined stance to reclaim land, and *Our Home Land is an Eternal Love Song*, which shows a female figure in traditional dress holding a pickaxe in her left hand, and in her right hand, above her head, an illustrative village scene of homes and vegetation. In this later poster, the village scene is replaced with the Palestinian national flag, a call perhaps to include women in the pursuit of liberation.

Real Australians Say Welcome
Peter Drew
2015, Australia

Adelaide-based street artist Peter Drew spent three months in 2015 pasting these posters around Australia, inspired by the second verse of the Australian national anthem: "For those who've come across the seas / We've boundless plains to share / With courage let us all combine / To advance Australia fair." The posters showed support for refugees and asylum-seekers in a country where anti-immigrant racism is rife, and offshore detention centers used to hold refugees have been routinely criticized for their human rights abuses. Drew wheat-pasted more than 1,000 posters in key cities around Australia and asked others for help distributing in more rural areas. The project was entirely crowdfunded. In 2017, the posters were modified to acknowledge Australia's indigenous communities with the refrain: "Real Australians *Seek* Welcome," in reference to a time prior to European invasion, when Australia's native communities acknowledged each other's land ownership by seeking welcome.

"Alan and Gyan"
Pete Reynolds for
Amnesty International
2016, UK

In the midst of a mountainous landscape, two silhouettes, backlit with a luminous yellow, can just be seen. The figures appear to be in wheelchairs, incongruous given the surrounding rocky and rugged terrain. Toward the bottom left of the poster, two lines of text provide both context and confirmation of the wheelchairs' presence, and from the flat colors and shadows of the poster, the miraculous story of Alan and Gyan emerges: "A brother and sister who fled Syria in wheelchairs, conquered mountains determined to find safety." Designed by British-based illustrator Pete Reynolds, the poster was one in a series of three produced for Amnesty's i-welcome—a campaign in support of refugee rights and to counter populist rhetoric that discriminates against refugees.

> **"IT IS THE OBLIGATION OF EVERY PERSON BORN IN A SAFER ROOM TO OPEN THE DOOR WHEN SOMEONE IN DANGER KNOCKS."**
>
> *Dina Nayeri*
> IRANIAN AMERICAN NOVELIST

No One Is Illegal
Diptych
Josh MacPhee,
Justseeds
2016, USA

Comprising two posters —"No Wall Unclimbed" and "No Fence Uncut"— this diptych was designed in support of resistance to controlling people's movements. Josh MacPhee explains: "People move. This is a reality, plain and simple. It is criminalized and made painful, and even lethal, by the borders created by states, capitalism, and xenophobes." The tag "No one is illegal" references the notion that declaring a human being illegal is in itself an illegal act by fact of the Universal Declaration of Human Rights (UDHR), which states that not only does everyone have the right to freedom of movement, but the right to a nationality and the right to seek asylum. However, under the International Covenant on Civil and Political Rights (ICCPR)—a companion to the UDHR—governments may restrict movement for reasons such as public safety, health, and order. This clause is often cited as justification of legal frameworks that many believe mask racist and oppressive policies, and the subsequent language used to describe immigrants, i.e. "illegal," further criminalizes them.

THE ART OF PROTEST   29

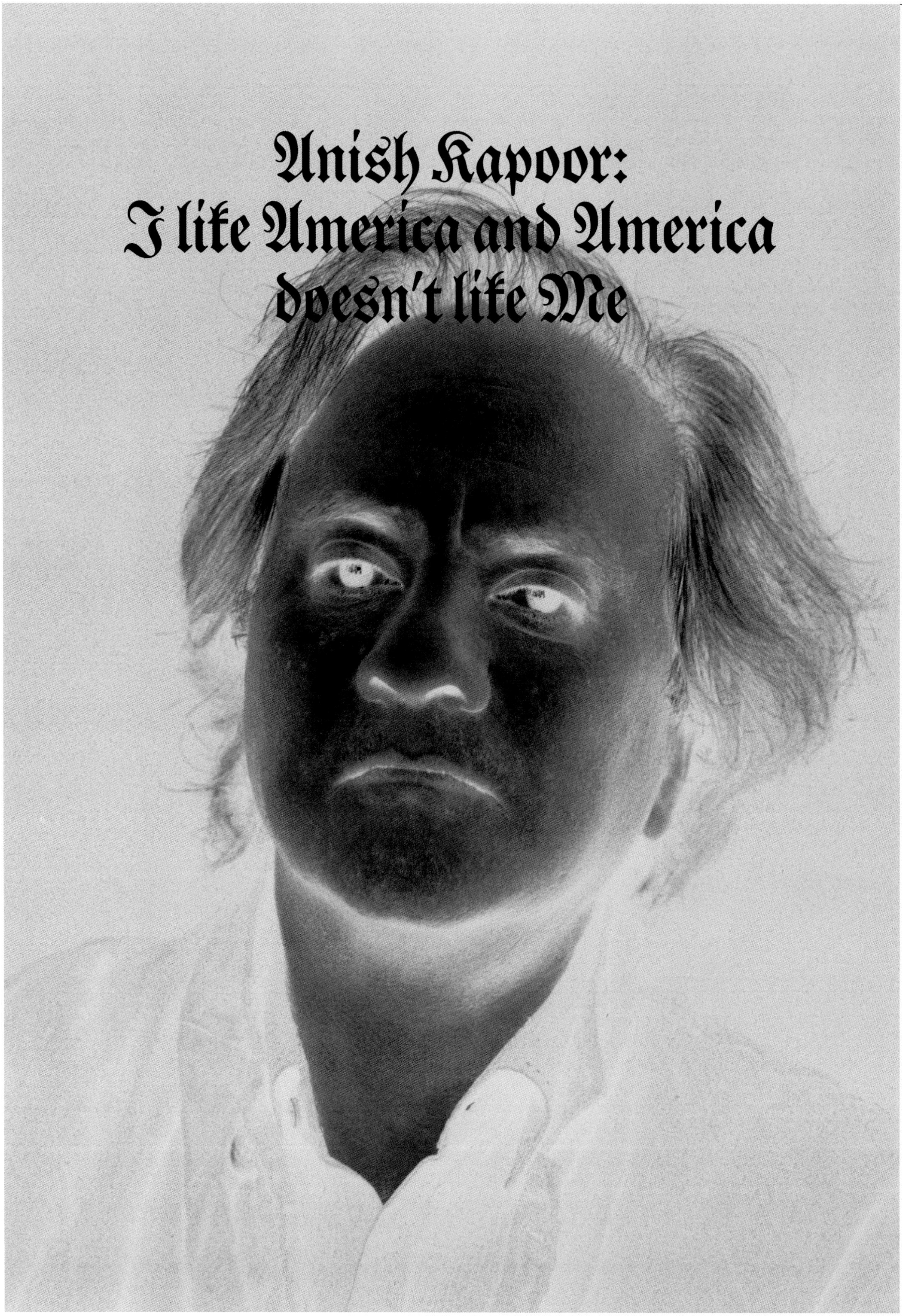

I Like America and America Doesn't Like Me
Anish Kapoor
2017, UK

British-Indian artist Anish Kapoor created this protest image in response to the Donald Trump administration; ten days after taking office, Trump restricted entry to the US for those with origins in Muslim-majority countries. Featuring a font evocative of Nazi propaganda and a photograph of Kapoor, the poster takes inspiration from the poster for Joseph Beuys's performance piece—*I Like America and America Likes Me* (1974). Kapoor called on others to do the same, saying: "I call on fellow artists and citizens to disseminate their name and image using Joseph Beuys's seminal work of art as a focus for social change. Our silence makes us complicit with the politics of exclusion. We will not be silent."

"MEN BUILD TOO MANY WALLS AND NOT ENOUGH BRIDGES."

Joseph Fort Newton
AMERICAN BAPTIST MINISTER, AUTHOR, AND HISTORIAN

No Ban, No Wall
Amnesty International
2017, USA

Protesting two issues simultaneously, this poster from Amnesty USA tackles Trump policies that have one primary and unitary aim—to keep immigrants out of the United States. A week after inauguration, on Holocaust Memorial Day, Trump signed an executive order banning travel to the US from seven Muslim-majority countries—Iraq, Syria, Iran, Libya, Somalia, Sudan, and Yemen—earning it the unofficial title of the "Muslim ban." The building of the wall between Mexico and the US (in truth, the completing; there is already a border wall) was a signature promise of Trump's election campaign. His determination to see it through sparked the lengthiest government shutdown in US history and saw Trump declare a national emergency in a bid to secure funding; the majority of Americans, including every congress member along the southern border, do not want it. This poster is part of a larger, ongoing campaign with coordinated tactics such as banner flyovers, protest message projections onto government buildings, and online petitions. The familiar yellow backdrop and block font makes the poster instantly recognizable as Amnesty, and its simplicity means it can be shared easily and quickly via social media, ensuring a greater dissemination.

"REMEMBER, REMEMBER ALWAYS, THAT ALL OF US, AND YOU AND I ESPECIALLY, ARE DESCENDED FROM IMMIGRANTS AND REVOLUTIONISTS."
Franklin D. Roosevelt
US PRESIDENT AND SOCIAL REFORMER

Defend DACA
Ashley Lukashevsky
2017, USA

This poster from Hawaiian-born illustrator Ashley Lukashevsky protests President Trump's scrapping of the Deferred Action for Childhood Arrivals (DACA), a program introduced in 2012 by Barack Obama that temporarily protects DREAMERs from deportation; DREAMERs is a term used to describe undocumented children who were brought to America illegally by their parents and who now live and go to school in the United States. It takes its name from the Development, Relief, and Education for Alien Minors Act (DREAM), which would offer a path to permanent citizenship, but also describes their hopes for a better future. Under the hashtag "#DefendDACA," three young students sit crossed-legged and with linked arms. From beneath them, roots grow deep into the earth, symbolizing their intrinsic connection to their homeland, the United States. Two of them wear graduation caps and gowns while one wears a t-shirt that says "This is home." Lukashevsky shares her art widely on social media to inspire action and promote a sense of community.

Family Separations
Boys + Girls Advertising Agency with illustration by Noma Bar
2018, Ireland

With his instantly recognizable signature style of flat, bold colors and minimal detail, Noma Bar's poster for Amnesty International powerfully connects the viewer with the horrors of family separations that took place in 2018 at the US-Mexico border. Sanctioned by President Trump, thousands of children were removed from their families by the American authorities and held in prisonlike rooms, their parents criminally prosecuted for crossing the border. Constructed from the elements of the American flag—a symbol of the "land of the free"—the red stripes on the poster become bars of a cage, behind which is a child's face, seen in profile and rendered in blue. The child appears to be crying as a single tear falls from its star-shaped eye. In subverting the flag, Bar effectively transformed the ensign from a symbol of national pride to one of shame. Although Trump made a U-turn on his controversial policy after fierce national backlash, many children still remain separated from their parents.

WOMEN ARE LIKE TEABAGS. YOU DON'T KNOW HOW STRONG THEY ARE UNTIL YOU PUT THEM IN HOT WATER.

Eleanor Roosevelt

HUMANITARIAN AND WIFE OF FRANKLIN D. ROOSEVELT

"Bugler Girl"
Caroline Marsh Watts, Artist's Suffrage League (ASL)
1908, UK

Designed for a rally by the National Union of Women's Suffrage Societies (NUWSS) in response to Prime Minister Herbert Asquith's challenge that British women should prove that they wanted the vote, this poster features an image of the "Bugler Girl." Although the depiction evokes Boudicca-like characteristics—notably the tumbling, tawny-hued hair, armor, and bugle held aloft in rallying war cry—the NUWSS was keen to emphasize that they were a nonmilitant organization, saying: "Our Bugler Girl carries her bugle and her banner; her sword is sheathed by her side; it is there, but not drawn, and if it were drawn, it would not be the sword of the flesh, but of the spirit. For ours is not a warfare against men, but against evil . . ." Nevertheless, she is the antithesis of domesticity, depicted standing firmly atop her castle, summoning others to join the fight for equality, the rising sun in the background symbolic of a new era dawning. Reportedly, up to 13,000 women marched from the Embankment in central London to the Royal Albert Hall on June 13, 1908. A peaceful protest, it paved the way for others, and the "Bugler Girl's" popularity traveled the Atlantic to become an iconic image of the suffrage movement in the United States as well.

The Cat and Mouse Act
The Women's Social and Political Union (WSPU)
1913, UK

Refused the right to be recognized as political prisoners, many suffragettes who had been jailed for vandalism, committed in support of women's suffrage, staged hunger strikes. After public outrage at these women being force-fed, the Prisoners (Temporary Discharge for Ill-health) Act, 1913 was introduced. It meant that women on hunger strike could be released from prison because of ill health, but could then be reimprisoned once they had recovered. This process, of release and then recapture, earned the measure the popular title of "The Cat and Mouse Act," because of its similarities to the way a cat will play with its prey before killing it. The poster features a fierce cat with a frail-looking woman dangling from its jaws. Behind is a darkened London skyline with lights on in the Tower of London. After the act's introduction, force-feeding was abandoned, allowing the government to claim that any harm (or even death) as a result of starvation was entirely the fault of the suffragette. Rather than give the government moral authority, the act strengthened the suffragettes' cause, and the general public began to view them as victims rather than vandals. In addition, the reality of recapturing these women was fraught with problems, not least because underground suffragette networks helped women elude rearrest.

THE ART OF PROTEST 37

"ANY WOMAN WHO CHOOSES TO BEHAVE LIKE A FULL HUMAN BEING SHOULD BE WARNED THAT THE ARMIES OF THE STATUS QUO WILL TREAT HER AS SOMETHING OF A DIRTY JOKE. THAT'S THEIR NATURAL AND FIRST WEAPON. SHE WILL NEED HER SISTERHOOD."
Gloria Steinem
FEMINIST, WRITER, AND ACTIVIST

What a Woman may be, and yet not have the Vote
Suffrage Atelier
c. 1913, UK

The Suffrage Atelier was an artist collective that worked "to advance the women's movement, and particularly the Enfranchisement of Women, by means of pictorial publications." Formed in 1909, in Shepherd's Bush, west London, by playwright Laurence Housman, his sister, artist Clemence Housman, and Alfred Pearse, a political cartoonist, the Suffrage Atelier also ran printmaking workshops and organized competitions for its members to submit work for use in the campaign. Posters were block-printed from simple woodcuts and then colored by hand, meaning they could be created cheaply and quickly. In this poster, a series of "worthy" females including nurse, mayor, and doctor are juxtaposed with "unworthy" male counterparts such as drunkard and convict. Viewing the poster today, it is hard to argue in favor of the absurdity of the system of the time, and denying women the right to vote.

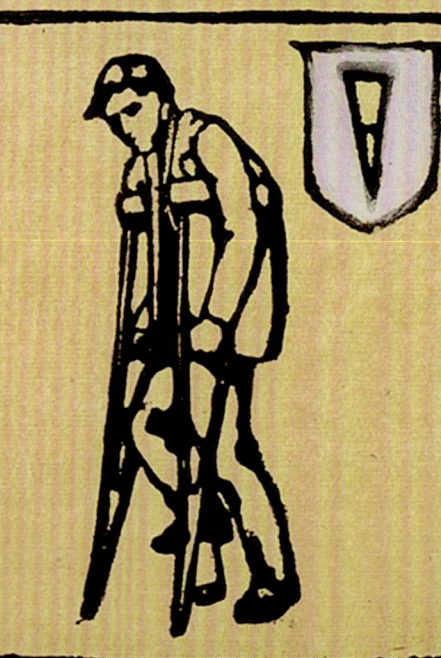

Let Ohio Women Vote
Cornelia Cassady Davis
c. 1913, USA

Painted by Cornelia Cassady Davis, an American artist best known for her portraits of Native Americans, this poster uses the seal of the state of Ohio as a foundation on which to campaign for women's suffrage. A young woman, head tilted slightly skyward, stands in front of three hilltops over which the sun is rising. In the foreground, a shaft of wheat (indicative of Ohio's farming background) and a clutch of arrows (symbolic of Ohio's Native Americans) frame the woman. The hills and sun offer an angelic appearance to the woman by seeming to form wings and a halo. The sun rising was a common symbol used in women's suffrage to depict a new era dawning: "Let Ohio Women Vote," says the poster. In the US, many campaigned for women's suffrage at state level to change laws prohibiting women from voting. The Ohio Woman Suffrage Association stood out from others as it actively encouraged African American women to join its cause and included those previously ignored at state level. Some women in the US achieved the right to vote in 1920, following the passing of the Nineteenth Amendment to the Constitution. Ohio was the fifth state to ratify this amendment.

Heraus mit dem Frauenwahlrecht
Karl Maria Stadler, 1914, Germany

Produced just prior to the outbreak of the First World War, this poster calls for women to be granted the right to vote and reads: "Until now, prejudice and reactionary attitudes have denied full civic rights to women, who as workers, mothers, and citizens wholly fulfil their duty, who must pay their taxes to the state as well as the municipality. Fighting for this natural human right must be the firm, unwavering intention of every woman, every female worker. In this, no pause for rest, no respite is allowed. Come all, you women and girls, to the ninth public women's assembly on Sunday 8 March 1914, at 3 pm." At the center, a woman holds aloft a red flag that curls behind her (at the time it was mostly left-wing political parties such as the Social Democrats who supported women's rights). Her stature is mighty and commanding, and her feet, rather large and unshod, give her a medieval appearance. Following the end of the First World War, women were granted the right to vote in Germany (Weimar Republic) from November 12, 1918.

Give Mother the Vote. We Need It.
Rose Cecil O'Neill
1915, USA

This poster was designed by American artist and illustrator Rose Cecil O'Neill for the National Woman Suffrage Publishing Company. At the time, O'Neill was the country's highest-paid illustrator—male or female—thanks to her brainchild, the "Kewpies," cherubic baby figures that first appeared in a comic strip in *Ladies' Home Journal* in 1909. Kewpies became an international craze, and O'Neill capitalized on their popularity, using her wealth and influence to campaign on behalf of women's suffrage. This poster shows five of these Kewpies in booties, bonnets, and bibs, marching, with the head Kewpie holding aloft a banner reading: "Votes for Our Mothers." By appealing on behalf of mothers, the poster's message immediately presents an alternative to the stereotypical image of the suffragette as militant and antimen. The verse, also written by O'Neill, supports this message and asks why women, masters of social and domestic tasks, are not permitted to vote on issues that primarily affect them. On the left, next to a Kewpie's foot, is O'Neill's signature. She often used a quirky way of signing off to match her artwork, and this one seems to be joining the march.

"EACH TIME A WOMAN STANDS UP FOR HERSELF, WITHOUT KNOWING IT POSSIBLY, WITHOUT CLAIMING IT, SHE STANDS UP FOR ALL WOMEN."

Maya Angelou
WRITER, SINGER, AND CIVIL RIGHTS ACTIVIST

The repeal of the Napoleonic Code
Ligue d'Action Feminine
1926, France

Either side of an aged and ailing Napoleon, who is depicted as the Napoleonic Code personified, a rallying call reads "French women have Napoleon, purveyor of battlefields, to thank for the code that oppresses them. Join feminists to demand a repeal . . . it is more than a century late." The Napoleonic Code was a series of civil laws passed in 1804 to replace previous feudal laws and royal privileges. It was subsequently adopted across much of Europe and Latin America and still exists today, albeit with revisions. Although its main purpose was to modernize, the new laws advocated for the supremacy of men, meaning woman had few rights. Napoleon was reported to have declared: "Women ought to obey us. Nature has made women our slaves!" The code ensured that men had the legal right to control women. Married women, in particular, owed their husband obedience and were forbidden from selling, giving, mortgaging, or buying property. It was a major setback for women's rights, which not only affected women in France, but reverberated with repercussions for women throughout Europe as Napoleon made military gains across much of the continent. It wasn't until 1945 that French women won the right to vote, 1965 until they could work without their husband's permission, and 1970 before women in France gained full autonomy and independent citizenship.

THE ART OF PROTEST 43

Russian Women's Day Poster
Boris Nikolayevich Deykin
1932, Russia

In January 2017, Russia did not hold a Women's March, unless you count sole protester Loretta Marie Perera. Yet one hundred years earlier, in 1917, more than 100,000 women helped spark the Russian Revolution, which paved the way for a new government and a country that was at the forefront of early twentieth-century feminism. In the same year, Soviet women gained the right to vote and, in 1920, Russia became the first country to legalize abortion (although it was banned again between 1936 and 1955). It was the norm for women to get an education, and expected that they should work. However, a common joke at the time was: *Under capitalism, women are not liberated because they have no opportunity to work. They have to stay at home, go shopping, do the cooking, keep house, and take care of the children. But under socialism, women are liberated. They have the opportunity to work all day and then go home, go shopping, do the cooking, keep house, and take care of the children.* The poster here reads: "8 March: A day of rebellion by working women against kitchen slavery. Say no to the oppression and vacuity of housework!" It shows a woman extending her hand to help another woman escape from under a heap of pots, pans, and other objects of domesticity.

National Conference of the CGT (Confédération Générale du Travail)
1958, France

This poster from 1958 invites women to join the CGT's conference and put forward their calls for equality, including a pay rise, equal pay for the same work (as men), two days of consecutive rest, maternity leave, and peace of mind. The illustration features two women—a factory worker and an office administrator—the two main domains of women in paid employment at the time. The portrayals are ideologically feminine—small waists, pert bosoms, and dainty shoes (not fit for the job in the case of the factory worker, who holds a wrench in her right hand!)—and expose the obstacles women faced in their quest for emancipation, namely the image of what a woman should be. CGT is a French workers' union. It was heavily male dominated, and getting women to join was a challenge. Women who did work were generally regarded as inferior to men, and in terms of equality, social reforms outranked economic in importance. Added to this, women were still bound by the traditional image of woman as domestic caregivers and actively encouraged to stay at home and have babies; even before the Second World War, France had suffered a declining birth rate. As Charles de Gaulle put it: *"en dix ans, douze millions de beaux bébés pour la France"* ("twelve million babies for France in ten years").

Un enfant . . . si je veux . . . quand je veux.
Mouvement Francais Pour Le Planning Familial (MFPF)
1970s, France

Produced during what has since become known as second-wave feminism, this poster and its slogan capture the essence of women's struggles through the 1960s and 1970s—namely the fight for a woman's autonomy and reproductive rights. Created by the MFPF, the poster features three generations of women in profile, and reads: "a child . . . if I want . . . when I want." The MFPF formed in 1960 and initially operated secretly; both abortion and contraception had been made illegal in France in 1920, in part to help boost birth rates following the First World War. It provided centers where women could access contraception that, although prohibited from sale, had been smuggled from England. Its success paved the way for the legalization of contraception in 1967. Following this, the MFPF worked with other like-minded organizations and activists under the banner of the Mouvement de Libération du l'Avortement et de la Contraception (MLAC), formed in 1973, and organized demonstrations in favor of free and legal contraception and abortion. France eventually passed an abortion law on January 17, 1975. It is known as the Veil Law after Simone Veil, who was a key figure in its ratification.

Parity Begins at Home
Pen Dalton, Women's Posters Brighton
1974, UK

This poster by artist Pen Dalton plays on the proverb "Charity begins at home." With its muted color palette and organic forms, the artwork takes its cue from art nouveau posters with one important difference. The female form often took center-stage in art nouveau design, depicted as empowered and breaking away from traditional roles. In this poster, the woman, although the central figure, is apron-clad and laden with a tray of refreshments that she is about to serve to her husband, who lounges on a comfortable chair. She stands with her hand on her hip, and her stance and expression suggest she is tired and fed up. During the 1970s, increasing numbers of women were entering the workplace, yet they were often paid much less than men and also expected to undertake domestic duties. This poster presents a powerful message about the importance of ensuring equality at home in the quest for women's liberation. Without freeing women from unpaid domestic servitude, true equality was unachievable.

THE ART OF PROTEST 47

Feminist Manifesto
Giò Tavaglione
1976, Italy

Feminism came to Italy later than other western countries, due mainly to Mussolini's Fascist government ruling for much of the first half of the twentieth century, Fascist ideology proclaiming it a woman's duty to procreate. It wasn't until the student movements of 1968 swept much of Europe that Italy's fight for equality and sexual liberation really took off. At the same time, an underground creative movement spawned several counterculture newspapers and magazines that promoted reform and freedom from repressive ideologies. This particular poster captures the spirit and struggle of 1970s feminism in Italy. Pope Paul VI, head of the Catholic Church at the time, is depicted with his hand held as if to physically halt the coming change. A procession of women's legs tramp across the top of the page, crushing church spires in their wake. At the center a naked woman plays an accordion, with the words "Aborto, Libero, Gratuito, Assistito" calling for free access to abortion. Other women, some clothed, some not, hold hands and dance out from the page. The poster is drawn together by the female gender symbol, at the bottom of which a lone woman kicks away a corkscrew, and is encircled with the words: "Non C'e Rivoluzione Senza Liberazione Della Donna . . . Non C'e' Liberazione Della Donna Senza Rivoluzione/ There Is No Revolution Without Women's Liberation . . . There Is No Women's Liberation Without Revolution."

Stop Forced Sterilization
People's Press
c. 1974, USA

Featuring three women of color with fists raised defiantly, this poster reads: "Stop Forced Sterilization," in both English and Spanish. The smaller text at the bottom of the poster presents startling information on the prevalence of sterilization in Puerto Rico, the US, and India. It surmises: "Too many people is not the problem; . . . US imperialism is the problem." Since a US-funded program was introduced in 1968, Puerto Rico has the highest rate of sterilization in the world. Many women thought the procedure was temporary or reversible; others were not even aware they were being sterilized. It didn't just happen in Puerto Rico. The US had been an early proponent of sterilization, with eugenics practiced long before Nazi Germany, and research shows an overwhelming incidence in black, Native American, and Latina women. Raising awareness of forced sterilization helped in part to give rise to the concept of reproductive justice. What this poster also exposes is the difference in experience that women of color had within the women's rights movement of the 1960s and 1970s: while white woman took to the streets to demand the right to abortion, many women of color were being denied the right to choose to have children.

Defenders of Women's Rights
Amnesty International
1994, Egypt

This poster says "Amnesty International is defending human rights" and was published by Amnesty International Egypt as part of an international campaign for women's rights: human rights are women's rights. It shows a photograph of a flower superimposed on the profile of a young woman's face. Women in Egypt have a long history of fighting for equality against what many see as a patriarchal system. In recent years some of its most prominent campaigners have been threatened by the government and charged with false crimes in an attempt to deter them from challenging the system. The prevalence of violence against women is also high, with incidents of mass sexual assault used as a tactic to deter women protesters, as well as frequent honor killings and widespread practice of female genital mutilation (FGM). In a 2013 poll, Egypt ranked worst for women's rights out of all Arab states. The flower in this poster is in bloom, with the pistil (the center of the flower containing the female reproductive organs) the focus, perhaps serving as a call to nurture and care for women.

Genital Mutilation
Red Pepper Posters
1980, USA

Against a striped background of black, tan, and white, an African woman in a headscarf is depicted in profile, with a younger girl of a different race in front of her. The poster was produced by Red Pepper Posters, a Bay Area collective started in San Francisco in 1976 by Barbara Morgan, who had previously worked with the Chicago Women's Graphics Collective. The text describes the effects of female genital mutilation (FGM) and ends: "In solidarity with African women and all women: that every woman may own her own body." FGM is primarily performed on young girls in Africa, although the poster's text also points out that clitoridectomy was used until fairly recently in the United States to treat hysteria, erotomania, and lesbianism. Up until the 1980s, the practice was primarily referred to as female circumcision, similar to male circumcision, and some opponents to the anti-FGM movement have criticized the use of the word "mutilation" as a subconscious aligning of nonwestern cultures with barbarism.

> "I AM NOT FREE WHILE ANY WOMAN IS UNFREE, EVEN WHEN HER SHACKLES ARE VERY DIFFERENT FROM MY OWN."
> *Audre Lorde*
> POET AND POLITICAL ACTIVIST

100 Years of International Women's Day
Favianna Rodriguez in collaboration with Syracuse Cultural Workers
2011, USA

International Women's Day (IWD) was first honored on March 19, 1911, when more than one million women and men across Austria, Denmark, Germany, and Switzerland united in a campaign calling for basic human rights for women. Today it is celebrated around the world on March 8 in recognition of progress made and of the many achievements by women, but also as a continued demand for equality. 2011 saw the hundredth anniversary of IWD, and this poster was one of two designed by Favianna Rodriguez in commemoration of women who work to bring communities together. The poster here shows a Latina worker rallying her community in support of immigrant rights. In the background is the female figure of Mother Earth, representing women everywhere. The text is in both English and Spanish, and toward the bottom includes contextual information on IWD. The sun behind Mother Earth has been a common motif used to symbolize a new dawn since the early twentieth-century suffrage campaigns, as has the color purple.

Women Should . . .
Memac Oglivy & Mather Dubai for UN Women 2013, Worldwide

Part of a series, this poster is based on genuine Google inquiries from March 9, 2013. The searches used Google's autocomplete function, which predicts results based on trends and previous searches. The results were shocking. From sexist statements to outright abuse, the returned searches exposed a global trend of systemic gender inequality. The poster design played on this grim realization by positioning the text of the search terms over the mouths of women of different races. It effectively emphasized that too often women don't have a say. The fact that, in 2013, blatant inequality could still exist made the series even more shocking. The campaign proved popular on social media; it was mentioned on Twitter twenty-four million times.

Adiós
Amnesty International
2018, Argentina and worldwide

The simple image of a coat hanger is all it takes to communicate the subject of this poster. A stark symbol long associated with unsafe abortion, the coat hanger appears on an all-green background—a color synonymous with woman's rights organizations since suffrage campaigns—with the word "Adiós." It appeared as an ad on the back of *The New York Times* international edition in 134 countries as a global show of solidarity and as a warning to Argentina's government that the world was watching. Despite a public movement in favor of decriminalizing abortion in Argentina, where currently it is only available if a women's life is in danger or the pregnancy is the result of rape, senators voted against the bill amid speculation that pressure from the Catholic Church had prevented its approval; Argentina is the homeland of Pope Francis. The national debate is ongoing. Unsafe abortions are Argentina's leading cause of maternal deaths, and have been for the past thirty years. In Latin America, only Cuba, Uruguay, and Mexico City have decriminalized abortion in all circumstances.

Respeta
Victoria García for Amplifier
2017, USA

For the Women's March in 2017, Amplifier—a design studio that helps grassroots movements get their message out—held an open call for artwork and received over 5,000 submissions in just eight days. "Respeta" was chosen as one of the five winning designs to become the official posters for the 2017 Women's March on Washington and was used in cities around the world. Thanks to digital downloads, dissemination of the posters was far and wide. The poster's text reads: "Respect my existence or expect resistance." It features a hybrid symbol of the female gender sign with a raised, clenched fist, often used to signify strength and solidarity in protest art. The way the poster's elements appear as if rubber-stamped intensifies the immediacy of the message. The Women's March took place on January 21, 2017, in protest at comments made by Donald Trump (whose inauguration was held the day before) that many felt were antiwomen. It started as a grassroots movement in Washington DC, which was the site of the main demonstration, with others organized across the world, from Antarctica to India. It was the largest single-day protest in US history.

> **"FEMINISM IS THE RADICAL NOTION THAT WOMEN ARE PEOPLE."**
> *Marie Shear*
> WRITER AND FEMINIST

ADIÓS

COMPLICATIONS FROM UNSAFE ABORTIONS ARE THE LEADING CAUSE OF MATERNAL DEATHS IN ARGENTINA.

ON AUGUST 8, SENATORS IN ARGENTINA COULD CHOOSE TO CHANGE THIS IF THEY VOTE THROUGH A BILL TO DECRIMINALIZE ABORTION.

THE WORLD IS WATCHING.

#AbortoLegalYa

Amnesty International

IF A BULLET SHOULD ENTER MY BRAIN, LET THAT BULLET DESTROY EVERY CLOSET DOOR.

Harvey Milk

CALIFORNIA'S FIRST OPENLY GAY ELECTED OFFICIAL

Homosexuals Are Different . . .
Mattachine Society of New York (MSNY)
c. 1960s, USA

One of the earliest gay rights organizations, the Mattachine Society, was founded by Harry Hay in 1950 in Los Angeles. Its name was adopted from the secret societies of masked men who fought social injustice in medieval France; an affinity Hay recognized with the cause of gay men in 1950s America. It existed as a national outfit until 1961, when it disbanded, by which time other chapters had formed across the US. Some, such as the publisher of this poster, stuck with the name. At the time this poster was produced, the gay rights movement was still nascent, and recruiting grassroots members was a primary aim of the MSNY. However, the group's choice of endearing animal drawings was a style that ultimately led to its demise. In 1969, the Stonewall riots charged the gay rights movement with a more radical and confrontational impetus. The MSNY was seen as too traditional and began to lose appeal. Its membership faded and the group split for good in 1987.

> "IT IS REVOLUTIONARY FOR ANY TRANS PERSON TO CHOOSE TO BE SEEN AND VISIBLE IN A WORLD THAT TELLS US WE SHOULD NOT EXIST."
> *Laverne Cox*
> ACTRESS AND ACTIVIST

Gay-in
Bruce Reifel for Gay Liberation Front
1970, USA

A silkscreen print with a very individualistic design, this poster reads: "Gay-In at Griffith Park merry-go-round, April 5—come together . . . reach out and join hands with your brothers and sisters." The artist features in the illustration (drawn center, with moustache) with his arms around another man, who has raised his fist. Predominantly pink, the poster has a joyful and jubilant tone. Its free form is indicative of the free-love era in which it was conceived. For gay people at the time, however, this freedom often meant under cover of night. Historically, Griffith Park in Los Angeles had been an after-dark cruising hotspot for gay men. But in 1968, the Gay Liberation Front took steps to give the local LGBTQ community a chance to celebrate and live life in the open with a festival held in the park during the day. It was an annual event for three years, and helped increase visibility and acceptance of LGBTQ people in LA. Ultimately it faced hostility from the police, especially in 1970, when they arrived dressed in riot gear.

St. Valentine's Revolutionary Emacipation (sic)
Brougham for the Gay Students' Union
1971, USA

The Stonewall riots of 1969 galvanized the gay rights movement in the US and gave rise to a number of organizations campaigning for change, two of which originated on the campus of the University of California, Berkeley, in San Francisco: The Gay Liberation Front (GLF) and the Students for Gay Power, which later changed its name to the Gay Students' Union. The GLF was arguably the more political, but in 1970, the Gay Students' Union organized the first authorized public gay dance at the Pauley Ballroom. Its success secured a second dance the following year, which is promoted by this 1971 poster: "St. Valentine's Revolutionary Emacipation (sic)." The main elements of the poster—a red heart, from which protrude yellow sun rays, fluffy white clouds, and a rainbow rising from green rolling hills, all set against a bright blue sky—work together to create a kaleidoscopic charm that captivates the viewer. The text also mentions "lights by Holy See," which must have been a draw, given that the lighting company was more often to be found staging psychedelic light shows for the Jimi Hendrix Experience, Pink Floyd, the Doors, and the Grateful Dead, among others.

Unite to Fight!
Donna Pillar for Inkworks Press
1976, USA

Originally published by Times Change Press, founded in 1970 by Su Negrin and Tom Wodetzki, Unite to Fight! features an image of a shouting figure inside a red-rimmed pink star that bleeds off all but one of the poster's edges. June 28 is a significant "day of solidarity with gay struggles" as it was the date the 1969 Stonewall riots began, for many the defining moment for change in America's history of gay rights. The halftone image of the human face was appropriated from another Times Change Press poster; as it was a women's rights poster published in 1970, the first edition of which credits Su Negrin as the designer, we can identify the individual as female. The poster here was first published in around 1973, a year before Times Change Press folded, and in 1976, Inkworks Press reprinted it.

LESBIANS AND GAYS SUPPORT THE MINERS
PRESENT

PITS AND PERVERTS

FEATURING

BRONSKI BEAT & GUESTS

AT THE ELECTRIC BALLROOM – CAMDEN

ON MONDAY 10TH DECEMBER –
8.P.M – 1.A.M.
(NR. TUBE: CAMDEN TOWN).

TICKETS – £4.50 (UNWAGED – £2.50)

AVAILABLE FROM:
"ROCK-ON RECORDS" 3 KENTISH TOWN RD. NW1.
OR "GAYS THE WORD" (BOOKSHOP) 66 MARCHMONT ST. WC1.
OR ALL RADICAL LONDON BOOKSHOPS.
ALL PROCEEDS WILL GO TO THE SOUTH WALES MINING COMMUNITY

POSTER DESIGN © KEVIN FRANKLIN.

Pits and Perverts
Kevin Franklin for London Lesbians and Gays Support the Miners (LGSM)
1984, UK

An unlikely union forged between two groups who on the surface could not appear more different —a small coal-mining community in south Wales and a London-based gay rights group (LGSM)—proved ultimately successful when LGSM raised more money for the striking miners than any other fundraiser in the UK. The LGSM saw an affinity between their struggles and those of the striking miners; both were marginalized groups fighting a right-wing press and a political elite who cold-shouldered their rights. Benefit concerts, such as the one advertised here (its title is a parody of tabloid headlines), helped raise the equivalent of $25,000 in today's money. A minibus was also provided to support the miners on their year-long strike—the longest in the UK since the general strike of 1926 and unsurpassed by anything since in terms of the scale of industrial action. In return, the Welsh miners marched alongside the LGSM at the 1985 Pride rally in London and supported motions for gay rights policy within the Labour Party.

Come Out . . . Come Out . . .
Jan Phillips, Amy Bartell, Susie Gaynes for Syracuse Cultural Workers
1987, USA

This poster features a large pink triangle as its backdrop. Towards the bottom edge there is a short history of this motif, explaining how it was reclaimed by the gay community as a symbol of pride, after its use by the Nazis as a "badge of shame" to identify gay men in the concentration camps. The main body text references the second National March on Washington for Lesbian and Gay Rights. This was a bigger success than the first in 1979, both in terms of attendance and outcomes, and is often referred to as "The Great March." Events of the 1980s had fueled the demand for more to be done in the fight for LGBTQ rights, the biggest of which was the growing AIDS crisis that was claiming the lives of gay men. The Reagan administration's lack of recognition and inaction on AIDS galvanized a large number of AIDS activists, who were prominent in the march. A year after this rally, the first National Coming Out Day was launched in commemoration, and to continue the momentum of the LGBTQ rights movement.

THE ART OF PROTEST 63

Silence=Death
Silence=Death Collective
1987, USA

Starting out as a six-person collective in New York City, Avram Finkelstein, Brian Howard, Oliver Johnston, Charles Kreloff, Chris Lione, and Jorge Soccarás conceived the poster "Silence=Death" amid growing concern about the AIDS epidemic within a largely politically silent environment. The poster was initially wheat-pasted around the streets of New York. Later, when the men joined the protest group Aids Coalition To Unleash Power (ACT UP), it was adopted and published by this organization. The pink triangle was inverted to point upward; both a reference to the Nazi genocide of gay men, which the Silence=Death group likened to that of the AIDS crisis, and a defiant stand against victimhood. After studying other contemporary campaigns, the creators chose a simple slogan to maximize its impact and to engage with multiple audiences. The mathematical representation also suggests that the text is irrefutable. The text at the bottom of the poster questions President Reagan's inaction on AIDS, and says: "What is really going on at the Center for Disease Control, the Food and Drug Administration, and the Vatican? Gays and lesbians are not expendable . . . Use your power . . . Vote . . . Boycott . . . Defend yourselves . . . Turn anger, fear, grief into action."

> **"WHY IS IT THAT, AS A CULTURE, WE ARE MORE COMFORTABLE SEEING TWO MEN HOLDING GUNS THAN HOLDING HANDS?"**
>
> *Ernest J. Gaines*
> AUTHOR AND EDUCATOR

A Little Too Straight
Laurie Casagrande for the Gay and Lesbian Community Action Council
1988, USA

This landscape-format poster features portraits of ten famous people whose sexual orientation was, at the time, omitted from history books. Its heading plays on the idiom of "setting the record straight" as well as the common term for referring to heterosexual people. The poster was produced by the Gay and Lesbian Community Action Council—now OutFront Minnesota—for the first National Coming Out Day in 1988, which was held a year after the National March on Washington for Lesbian and Gay Rights (see page 63). An annual observance every October 11, it was founded in the US by activists Robert Eichberg and Jean O'Leary and built on the principle that the most fundamental form of activism is coming out and living as an openly lesbian or gay person.

Dyke
Fierce Pussy
1991 (original) 2009 reproduction, USA

Fierce Pussy is a lesbian art collective borne out of the protest group ACT UP in response to a call to make lesbianism more visible at a time when AIDS activism was predominantly the domain of gay men. The image of a child above the typewritten word "Dyke," seen in a public space, aimed to reclaim derogatory language and increase the familiarity and representation of lesbians. The original poster was produced in 1991 on a photocopier at magazine publisher Condé Nast's offices (where some of the collective worked) and wheat-pasted around New York City. This working model of using readily available resources reflected both the urgency of Fierce Pussy's work and its covert nature (putting up posters being illegal at the time). However, their posters were reproduced in 2009 as part of an exhibition—*ACT UP New York: Activism, Art and the AIDS Crisis, 1987–1993* at Harvard's Carpenter Center—and recently were part of an installation at the Leslie-Lohman Museum of Gay and Lesbian Art, where the posters were enlarged and wheat-pasted onto the museum's windows.

Stonewall 25
Linda Malik and Dik Cool with art by Harry Freeman-Jones
1994, USA

Bedecked in the iconography of the gay liberation movement, this poster, with artwork from artist and activist Harry Freeman-Jones, commemorates the twenty-fifth anniversary of the Stonewall riots—a three-day rebellion in 1969, led by the gay community in New York, which many see as the catalyst for the modern LGBTQ rights movement in the US. Created with strips of colored paper, the rainbow flag, pink triangle, and less familiar lambda symbol (adopted in 1970 by Tom Doerr, an American gay activist, as the symbol of the New York chapter of the Gay Activists Alliance) adorn the upper half of the poster. Some of the pink triangles have been blackened, and the presence of the looped red ribbon to the left—the universal symbol of HIV and AIDS awareness—suggests also a commemoration of those lost to the disease. As the text says: "We will remember those who have died of hatred, whether by violence or by government inaction in the face of the AIDS epidemic."

25 YEARS AFTER STONEWALL

**STRONG IN DIVERSITY
STRONG IN SPIRIT
STRONG IN LOVE**

DENYING IGNORANCE & HATE POWER OVER OUR LIVES DEFYING BIGOTRY MASKED BY FALSE MORALITY EMBRACING THE TRUTH OF OUR BEING MEN LOVING MEN & WOMEN LOVING WOMEN AGAINST GENERATIONS OF LIES WE DECLARE WITH PRIDE THE GAY & LESBIAN AGENDA:

TO LOVE & BELOVED

"...recognition of the inherent dignity and of the equal and inalienable rights of all members of the human family is the foundation of freedom, justice and peace in the world."
—Preamble to the Universal Declaration of Human Rights

In the early hours of June 28, 1969, the police raided the Stonewall Inn in New York City's Greenwich Village. For the police, it was just another routine raid on a gay bar on Christopher Street. But this time, we fought back! The Stonewall Rebellion lasted for three days and nights — and no one could have imagined how they were changing the course of history. Suddenly, the ancient burden of oppression was transformed into anger, self-affirmation, pride — and ACTION!

The call for lesbian, gay, bisexual, drag and transgender liberation was heard around the world. Today, our movement ranks among the great forces in the struggle for human rights. On June 26, 1994, we will gather in diversity and solidarity — with many victories to celebrate and many injustices to protest. We will remember those who have died of hatred, whether by violence or by government inaction in the face of the AIDS epidemic. Our voices will be heard! Join us!

International *March* on the *United Nations* to *Affirm* the *Human Rights* of *Lesbian* and *Gay People*

JUNE 26, 1994   NEW YORK CITY

Charles Can Marry Twice
OutRage!
2005, UK

Referring to the 2005 marriage of Prince Charles to Camilla Parker Bowles, this poster protests the fact that he was allowed to marry for a second time (following his divorce from Princess Diana in 1996), yet gay people, at the time, were not legally able to marry at all. Although the UK's Civil Partnership Act came into effect on December 5, 2005, it wasn't until 2014 when same-sex marriages were made legal in England, Scotland, and Wales. The one-color production and newsstand-like appearance were familiar features of OutRage! posters; it was a style that ultimately suited their cause and their budget. Founded by volunteers, including human rights activist Peter Tatchell, OutRage! was a collective response to rising violence towards gay people in the UK and the surge in the number of gay and bisexual men arrested for consensual gay behavior. A direct-action group, OutRage! favored nonviolent but radical acts of civil disobedience, such as in September 1990, when the group organized a "kiss-in" at Piccadilly Circus to protest the arrests of gay men for kissing in public. It campaigned on issues of equality for twenty-one years, from 1990 until 2011.

> "THE ONLY QUEER PEOPLE ARE THOSE WHO DON'T LOVE ANYBODY."
> *Rita Mae Brown*
> WRITER, ACTIVIST, AND FEMINIST

Some People Are Gay. Get Over It!
Stonewall
2007, UK

Part of the "Get Over It!" series developed by Stonewall UK, this poster was designed to help tackle homophobic, biphobic, and transphobic bullying in schools. It was originally sent to every secondary school in England, but its impactful design lent itself well to other platforms, and it has since been seen on 600 billboards, on 20 major railway stations' advertising screens and on 3,500 bus panels across the UK. Stonewall, the largest LGBTQ rights organization in Europe, was originally formed in 1989 to lobby against Section 28—a law passed by then UK prime minister Margaret Thatcher that banned schools from discussing homosexuality and prohibited libraries from stocking gay or lesbian literature. It was the first new homophobic law in a century. Although it was later repealed (in Scotland on June 21, 2001, and in the rest of the UK on November 18, 2003), its damaging legacy remained, giving voice to hate and homophobia that is still being challenged today.

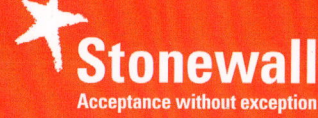

I love my boo.
Gay Men's Health Crisis (GMHC)
2008–10, USA

First produced in 2008, these posters were updated in 2010 and spotted across New York's subway, as well as shared on social media (for which the campaign won an award). They were pioneering in that they featured black and Latino gay men captured during moments of intimacy. The campaign's aim was to raise the profile of gay men of color and challenge negative stereotypes. The use of real people over the clichéd images of well-honed models usually seen in gay men's literature was central to the campaign and helped spur success on social media. In using relatable images, and promoting a message of affection and care, the posters also sought to encourage safer sex: black gay or bisexual men are still disproportionately affected by HIV and AIDS, with a lower percentage knowing their HIV status compared with HIV-positive gay and bisexual men of other ethnicities.

ACT UP 20 Ans
Tommy Knuts: Gobelins, l'École de l'image for ACT UP-Paris
2009, France

An all-black page with the profile of a phallic image at the center constructed from the words "ACT UP 20 Ans. Nous sommes au regret de vous annoncer les 20 ans d'ACT UP Paris/We regret to announce 20 years of ACT UP Paris," this poster suits the style of activism that ACT UP-Paris—which was founded in 1989 by three French journalists, Didier Lestrade, Pascal Loubet, and Luc Coulavin—is associated with: confrontational and militant. ACT UP-Paris is known for performing acts of rebellion, such as sheathing the obelisk on Paris's Place de la Concorde in a giant pink condom, or staging die-ins to bring attention to government inaction on AIDS and campaigning for LGBTQ rights in France. This poster was one of a series produced for the twentieth anniversary of ACT UP-Paris by students at a design school in the city: Gobelins, l'École de l'image. Of twenty submissions, three were chosen for distribution.

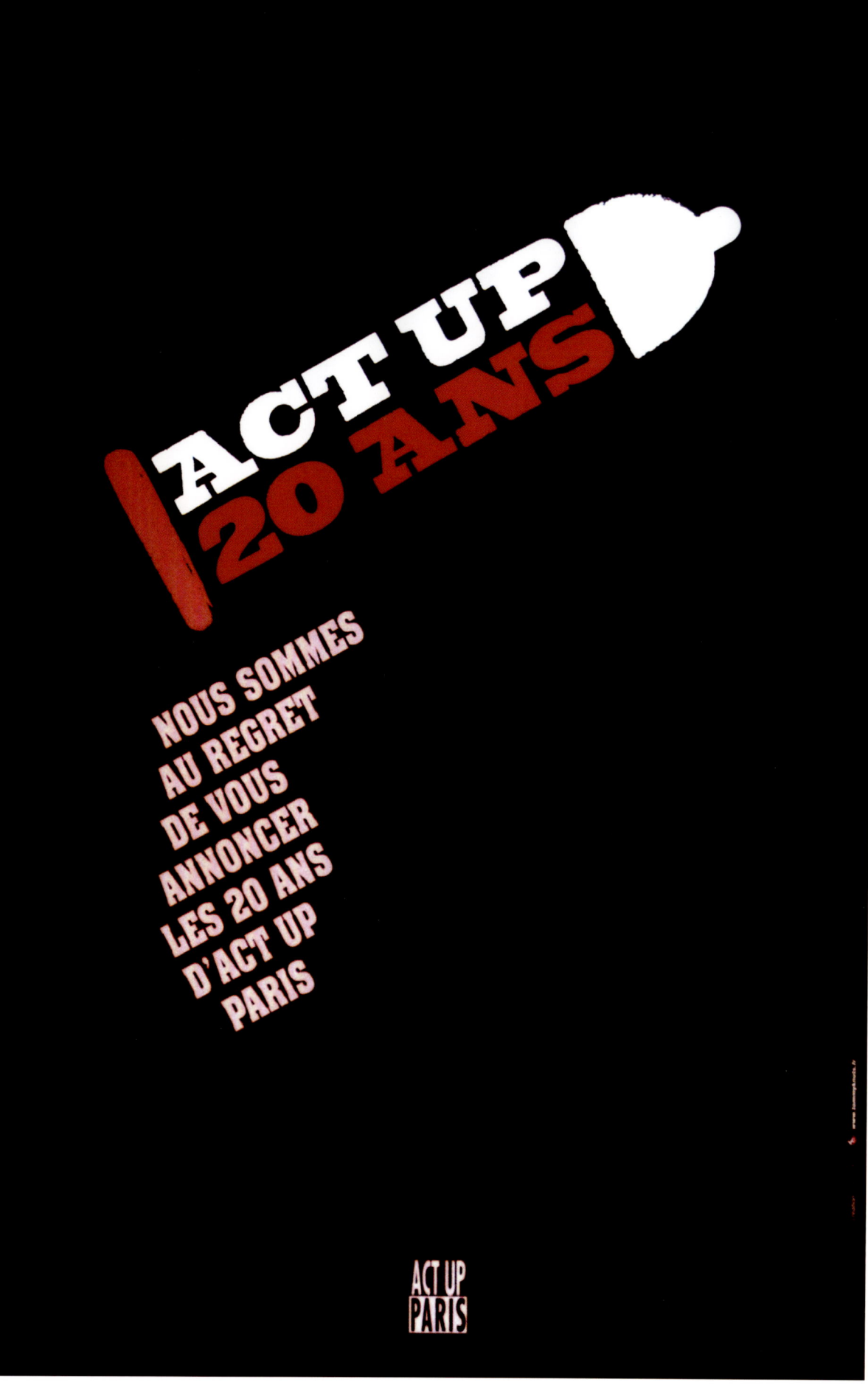

'YOUR SO

CAN YOU SPOT TWO COM

Gay. Let's get over it.

@stonewalluk   facebook.com/stonewalluk

GAY.'

ON MISTAKES?

"Your So Gay."
Stonewall
2013, UK

Following on from the original "Some People Are Gay." campaign, this was one of a series of three posters, issued to around half of all secondary schools in the UK, to help tackle homophobic language. Of the 1,600 pupils interviewed by Stonewall, the organization behind the posters, almost all said they had heard regular use of homophobic language, with the word "gay" used as an insult. The difference between *your* and *you're* is a common grammar mistake. The poster invites the viewer to identify "two common mistakes" to demonstrate how using a phrase like "you're so gay" can cause offense, perpetuating homophobic beliefs that being gay is somehow wrong. The campaign was aimed at teachers as much as schoolchildren and highlighted the need for further training in challenging homophobic language in schools.

"I BELIEVE ALL AMERICANS WHO BELIEVE IN FREEDOM, TOLERANCE AND HUMAN RIGHTS HAVE A RESPONSIBILITY TO OPPOSE BIGOTRY AND PREJUDICE BASED ON SEXUAL ORIENTATION."
Coretta Scott King
ACTIVIST AND WIFE OF MARTIN LUTHER KING, JR.

Trans Power
Collaboration with TransLatin@ Coalition and Rommy Torrico for Trans Day of Resilience
2015, USA

In 2015, the Transgender Day of Remembrance—a movement founded in 1999 in memory of Rita Hester, a transgender woman who was murdered in 1998 and, historically, a day to mourn others lost to transphobic violence—was expanded to include the Trans Day of Resilience as a way of also commemorating the strength of those living within the transgender community. The year 2015 witnessed increasing levels of violence against transgender and gender non-conforming people in the US and, according to the National Coalition of Anti-Violence Programs (NCAVP), predominantly against transgender women of color who accounted for more than half those murdered. The poster here juxtaposes the opposing themes of violence and virtue: an "angel" rises up from a darkened city labeled with hostile words such as fear, rape, and death. With a fist raised defiantly, the figure transcends this darkness, encircled by a halo of fortifying words written in both Spanish and English, toward a plaque festooned with flowers that reads, simply: "Trans Power."

Tšetšenia
Pekka Piippo for Amnesty International
2014, Finland

A reworking of the Russian coat of arms forms the basis of this poster protesting Vladimir Putin's regime, under which the rights and freedom of LGBTQ people in Russia have deteriorated. The two-headed eagle has turned upon itself, with one side of the conjoined creature slaughtering its other rainbow-hued half. The three crowns, symbols of unity and sovereignty, tumble to the side, and the once bicephalic figure becomes symbolically weaker. Although homosexuality was decriminalized in Russia in 1993, there has been an increase in human rights abuses in recent times. There are still no laws prohibiting discrimination based on sexual orientation, and the level of intolerance has been rising steadily amid an increasingly hostile environment. In 2013, Russia banned the promotion of "nontraditional" sexuality—broadly seen as an attack on gay rights—and 2017 bore witness to the violent persecution of gay men in Chechnya with dozens abducted, tortured, and killed.

Back Home, It's A Crime To Show My Colours
Fondation Émergence
2018, Canada

Since 2000, Fondation Émergence has campaigned against homophobia and transphobia, including initiating the International Day Against Homophobia and Transphobia (IDAHOT) in 2003. Each year, it organizes an awareness campaign, which for 2018 focused on rights around the world. This campaign produced a series of posters, each featuring a photograph of a lesbian, gay, or trans person wearing a rainbow flag—a symbol of pride for the gay community since the 1970s, when it was designed by American gay rights activist, Gilbert Baker (the different colors celebrating diversity). The poster uses the idiom "showing your colors" to demonstrate how, for many people around the world, being open can mean a criminal charge or worse. The man featured in this poster is from Tunisia, where people can serve up to three years in prison for being gay or lesbian.

Equality Is A Human Right
Amnesty International
2016, USA

The International Day Against Homophobia, Transphobia, and Biphobia takes place on May 17 each year. Although, overall, there has been progress in the pursuit of rights for LGBTQ people, there are still areas of concern. For example, 2015 saw a record number of documented murders of transgender Americans, mostly trans women of color. In the same year, gay men in Iraq and Syria plunged to their deaths after being pushed from rooftops on the orders of Islamic State. The following year, the deadliest act of violence against LGBTQ people in US history occurred when forty-nine people were massacred and fifty-three wounded at a gay nightclub in Orlando. Amnesty USA produced this graphic to help draw attention to human rights abuses like these. Its format and simple design allow it to be shared easily via social media platforms. As such, it can be disseminated quickly, not just to a wide audience but also to specific recipients such as government authorities and leaders of countries where LGBTQ people still face persecution or even death.

THOSE WHO LOVE PEACE MUST LEARN TO ORGANIZE AS EFFECTIVELY AS THOSE WHO LOVE WAR.

Martin Luther King, Jr.
BAPTIST MINISTER, NOBEL LAUREATE, AND CIVIL RIGHTS LEADER

The Survivors. Make War on War
Käthe Kollwitz
1923, Germany

Kathe Kollwitz, a German artist closely associated with expressionism, captured the plight of the working class throughout her work. She also featured mothers prominently. Both are evident in this poster which calls for a "War on war!" Originally commissioned by labor unions in Amsterdam, the poster centers on a mother who is tightly clutching three small children. On either side of her are more children, making seven in total. Behind stand injured and old men. The monochromatic charcoal drawing helps convey the harrowing sense of loss (Kollwitz herself had lost her son Peter during the First World War). The eyes of the mother are completely black; her head is more skull than human face. Yet against all the adversity that war brings—poverty, hunger, and death—this emaciated matriarch exudes an air of defiance and strength. She is literally the center, offering an anchor to those around her amid the permeating despair. Kollwitz died a few days before the end of the Second World War.

> "PEACE CANNOT BE KEPT BY FORCE. IT CAN ONLY BE ACHIEVED BY UNDERSTANDING."
>
> *Albert Einstein*
> GERMAN-BORN THEORETICAL PHYSICIST

Die Saat des Todes
John Heartfield
1937, Germany

Produced just prior to the outbreak of the Second World War, this photomontage from Dada artist John Heartfield forewarns the tragedy of fascism. Heartfield, who was born Helmut Herzfeld but anglicized his name to protest rising anti-British sentiment in Germany, was an early proponent of political photomontage, producing many that protested Nazism. When the Nazi Party took power in 1933, he fled to Czechoslovakia and then to England. He was in the top ten of the Gestapo's most wanted. The poster reads: "The Seed of Death. Where this sower goes through the land he reaps hunger, war and fire." A skeleton soldier scatters swastikas from a sling worn around his neck. As they hit the ground, they turn from white to black, suggesting the fallacy and danger of Nazi ideologies. In the background, a group of men wearing gas masks carry someone away on a stretcher under a dark sky filled with smoke.

Nie!
Tadeusz Trepkowski
1952, Poland

Designed by self-taught graphic designer Tadeusz Trepkowski, this postwar Polish poster is a succinct appeal for peace. Pared to the minimum, it features a single shard of a building licked by flames, within a silhouette of a bomb, and includes just one word: "Nie!" ("No!"). Poland suffered a great deal of damage during the Second World War, with much of Warsaw razed to the ground. The memory of this suffering resulted in a plethora of peace propaganda posters. As Poland was a satellite of the Soviet Union, this poster is all the more notable as it deviates from the socialist realism style that was prevalent at the time. Many of Trepkowski's posters feature the same, repeated motifs, such as the destroyed building seen here, and were remarkable for their use of objects rather than people to provoke emotion. Though Trepkowski died of a heart attack in 1954 at just forty years old, he is considered one of Poland's most influential poster designers.

Stop H-Bomb Tests
Ben Shahn for the National Committee
for a SANE Nuclear Policy
c. 1961, USA

The first successful hydrogen bomb (H-bomb) was detonated by the United States in November 1952. It was roughly a thousand times more powerful than the atomic bomb dropped on Hiroshima. Less than a year later, the Soviets exploded their first bomb. The nuclear arms race had started and, by the late 1970s, seven nations had built hydrogen bombs. At the time that this poster was produced, many Americans thought nuclear weapons essential to national security but did not consider, or were unaware, of the H-bomb's capacity for uncontrollable destruction. The core of this poster is a prominent black "blob" with a crudely drawn face. The "blob" has a monster-like appearance which could be an abstract representation of evil or the bomb-blast itself; or perhaps both. The typeface used is hand-drawn and its imperfectness hints at a human element, contrasting with the cold and calculated destruction offered by the H-bomb.

Vietnam Summer 1967
Artist unknown, 1967, USA

Vietnam Summer 1967 was a national campaign to bring about peace. Pioneered by the American Friends Service Committee (AFSC), a Quaker organization, it received support from Martin Luther King, Jr., and Benjamin Spock, among others. Posters were an important aspect of the campaign, particularly in uniting people in protest. Here, a terrified Vietnamese woman flees a background of flames—presumably a US napalm attack. We assume that she is a mother, as she holds what seem to be two young children. The way the children are held, and the jumbled tangle of limbs, evoke a sense of desperation and urgency while also implying the magnitude of the horror that she must escape. Throughout, the color in this poster is muted, tinged with darkness, as if the poster itself were caught in the attack, with smoke particles speckling the woman, children, and parts of the background, adding to the sense of confusion and disorientation. The first nationwide antiwar demonstrations took place across America in 1967.

Out of the Mouths of Babes
Personality Posters
Photography by Zabohonsk
Design by Graff
1970, USA

By 1970, many Americans wanted out of the Vietnam War. It had already claimed a huge human and financial cost, and doubts about victory were creeping in. The poster here features a photograph of a baby, staged like a studio portrait and shot against a bright-white background. In other circumstances it might have served as a cherished keepsake for a family album. Here, it sends an authentic and resolute statement about the hypocrisy of war: namely, drafting young men not yet old enough to vote. The baby stares wide-eyed at the viewer. In his hands he holds an inking stamp, and the inky smudges over his face and legs suggest this object has been handled with playful abandon. Yet printed across the baby's chest is the somber content of the stamp: "Bless those who declare war. They're usually too old, To fight and die."

War is not healthy for children and other living things ®
Lorraine Schneider for Another Mother for Peace
1969, USA

With its simple sunflower image and message this poster became an icon of the opposition to the Vietnam War. Designed by Lorraine Schneider, the image started life as a Mother's Day card; a group of concerned mothers sent a thousand cards to Washington, asking for "an end to killing" rather than "candy and flowers." This was the precursor to Another Mother for Peace—an organization set up "to educate women to take an active role in eliminating war as a means of solving disputes between nations, people and ideologies." Schneider was not a trained graphic designer—although she was an artist—and some argued that the poster was amateurish in execution. However, it held a universal truth that spoke to people and gave the anti-Vietnam War movement momentum. The logo was used on everything from bumper stickers to jewelry.

No Draft. No War. No Nukes.
Artist unknown
1970s–1980s, USA

Draft-card burning, a display of protest by conscientious objectors to the Vietnam War, was popular during the 1960s and 1970s in both the US and Australia. The first documented draft-card burning was by twenty-two-year-old Eugene Keyes in December 1963 in Illinois. By 1965, it was a frequent occurrence, and the US government enacted harsher laws in a bid to limit its influence. Australia also repressed such protest until the Labor government came to power and abolished conscription in 1972. President Richard Nixon put an end to the US draft in 1973. This pop art poster shows the world's most famous personification of freedom—the Statue of Liberty—holding aloft a burning draft card in protest at being conscripted to war, conveying a strong message about the right to personal freedom.

Bring The Monster Down, End the Air War
Doug Lawler, East Bay Media
1972, USA

This artwork is probably the most successful poster created by East Bay Media, set up in 1970 by artist Doug Lawler. Lawler himself designed this piece, which was left uncredited to preserve anonymity. It originally sold for two dollars. The style is typical of the time, reflecting both prevailing pop art influences as well as the resources that were available—East Bay Media first operated out of a small garage using donated and salvaged supplies. A menacing-looking eagle dominates the upper half of the poster, looming over three silhouettes of Vietnamese villagers working in the fields against a backdrop of flames. A twisting purple dragon occupies the lower part of the poster. Stylized lettering tops and tails the images. The poster protests America's "carpet-bombing" in Vietnam. The bald eagle, the national emblem of the United States, becomes a monster raining fire down on the Vietnamese. Given the significance of the dragon in Vietnamese folklore as a harbinger of rain, and as a symbol of the power of the nation, the purple dragon most likely portrays the growing Vietnamese resistance.

Till Aktion
Mika Launis for the
Finnish Peace Defenders
c. 1975, Sweden

Sweden signed the Treaty on the Non-Proliferation of Nuclear Weapons (NPT) in 1975. Although the country had maintained neutrality during the two world wars, it considered nuclear weapons a defense against a rising Soviet threat, and up until 1972 ran a clandestine nuclear weapons program. This poster is written in Swedish but was published by the Finnish Peace Defenders—Finland is a non-nuclear weapon state—and features an illustration by a Finnish artist. Sweden has a liberal political history, and this poster demonstrates how a country's political leaning can influence language. The words "Till Aktion mot upprustning!" communicate a leftist tone that calls on the masses to make a stand against nuclear weapons. The illustration echoes this sentiment by showing three young people drawn closely together. Their hands are linked and their shoulders overlap, suggesting others outside of the pastel drawing's parameters. A symbolic white dove with an olive branch in its beak, to which the female figure has turned her head, hovers over the group and accentuates the poster's message of peace.

It Will Be A Great Day
Women's International League for Peace and Freedom (WILPF)
1979, USA

This poster features a quote largely attributed to American author and minister Robert Lee Fulghum. Alongside the image of school-aged children playing on what appears to be a globe-shaped climbing frame, the typewritten text highlights how the US government at the time was spending more money on defense than education. As if to illustrate the point further, the poster is one-color and looks as if it is photocopied on low-grade paper. It was published by the Women's International League for Peace and Freedom (WILPF), a nongovernment organization of women working to promote peace and challenge governments that spend excessively on military defense. It was established in 1915, making it the world's oldest women's peace organization.

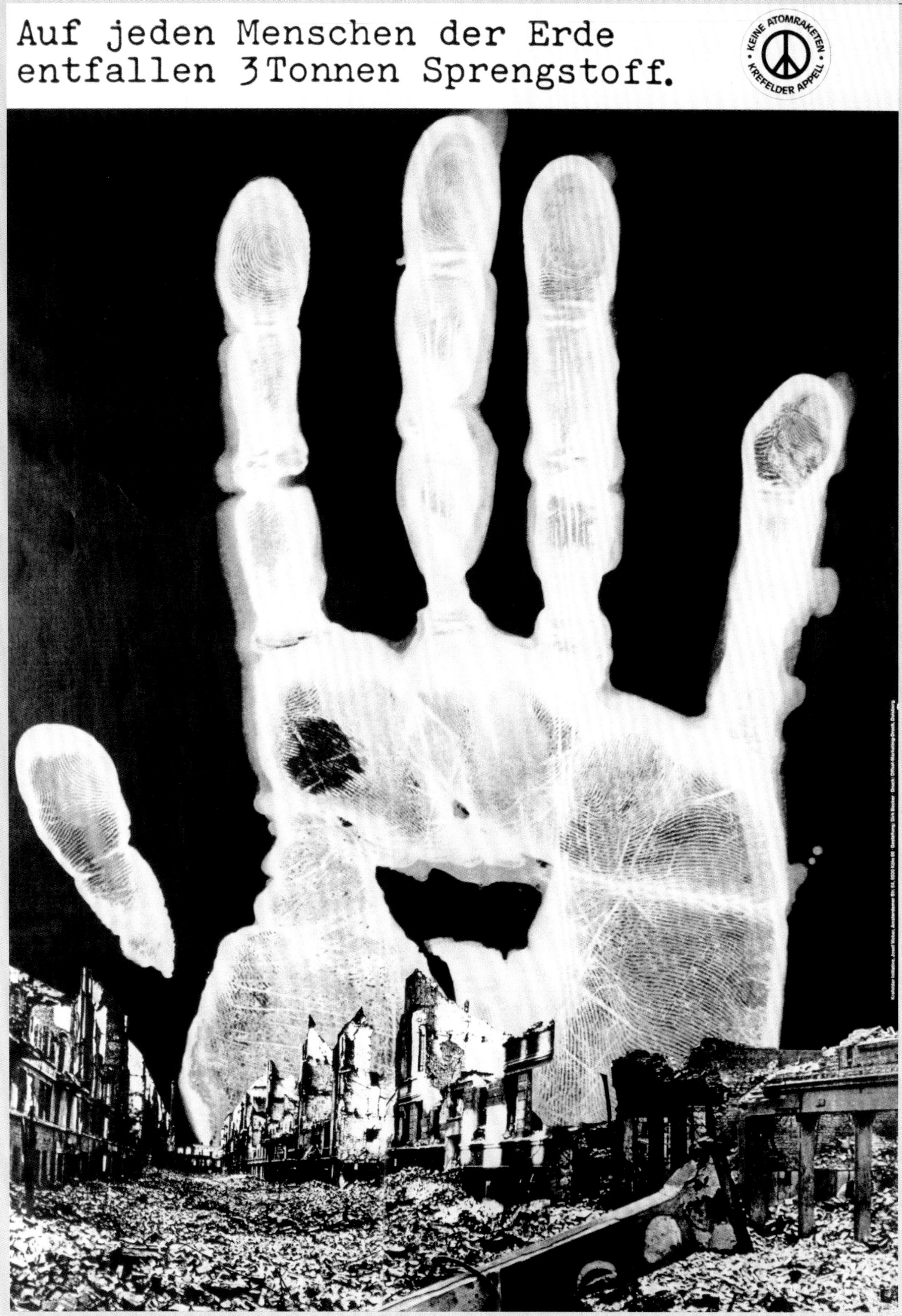

Auf jeden Menschen der Erde entfallen 3 Tonnen Sprengstoff.

KEINE ATOMRAKETEN · KREFELDER APPELL

Auf jeden Menschen der Erde entfallen 3 Tonnen Sprengstoff.
Dirk Becker for the
Krefelder Appell
1980, West Germany

This collage poster offers a view of an utterly destroyed street, littered with debris and half-standing buildings. Many of these appear residential, yet the only sign of human life is the giant negative handprint that dominates the blackened background. Almost X-ray-like in appearance, it is held up in a halting gesture, its ghostly look both a marker of radiation and a sign of human loss. The typewriter-like text on top reads: "Everyone on the earth is killed by three tons of explosives." The poster was produced in response to the NATO Double Decision of 1979, which offered the Warsaw Pact (whose growing nuclear capacity threatened Western Europe) a mutual limitation of medium-range and intermediate-range ballistic missiles, and that in a case of dispute, NATO would deploy more nuclear weapons in Western Europe. The theory was that if everyone had an equal capacity, then the threat would prevent the use. In 1980, peace activist Josef Weber initiated the Krefelder Appell to petition the German government to withdraw approval for the NATO decision and to end the arms race. By 1983, it had been signed by four million German citizens.

The hungry need bread not bombs. Stop the arms trade.
Quaker Peace & Service
1981, UK

With a core belief in pacifism, Quakers have often been at the forefront of campaigns for disarmament. They set up the Friends Peace Committee in 1888, became the Quaker Peace & Service in 1979, and are now known as the Quaker Peace and Social Witness. This poster appeals for an end to the arms trade. It was published during the era of the Second Cold War (1979–1985), when the world arms trade grew rapidly. The image is a very simple two-color illustration yet conveys a powerful message about the sometimes undocumented byproducts of war and forces a consciousness of opposition. At the head of the poster, a bomb, slightly cropped off the page and with a downward trajectory (suggesting detonation), is drawn sliced at one end. We can see that the inside is yellow, and the position of the wheat shaft, which is also yellow, directly beneath, visually transforms the bomb into a loaf of bread. Within the poster, the wheat shaft claims more space, leading us to deduce that food is more important to human survival than weapons.

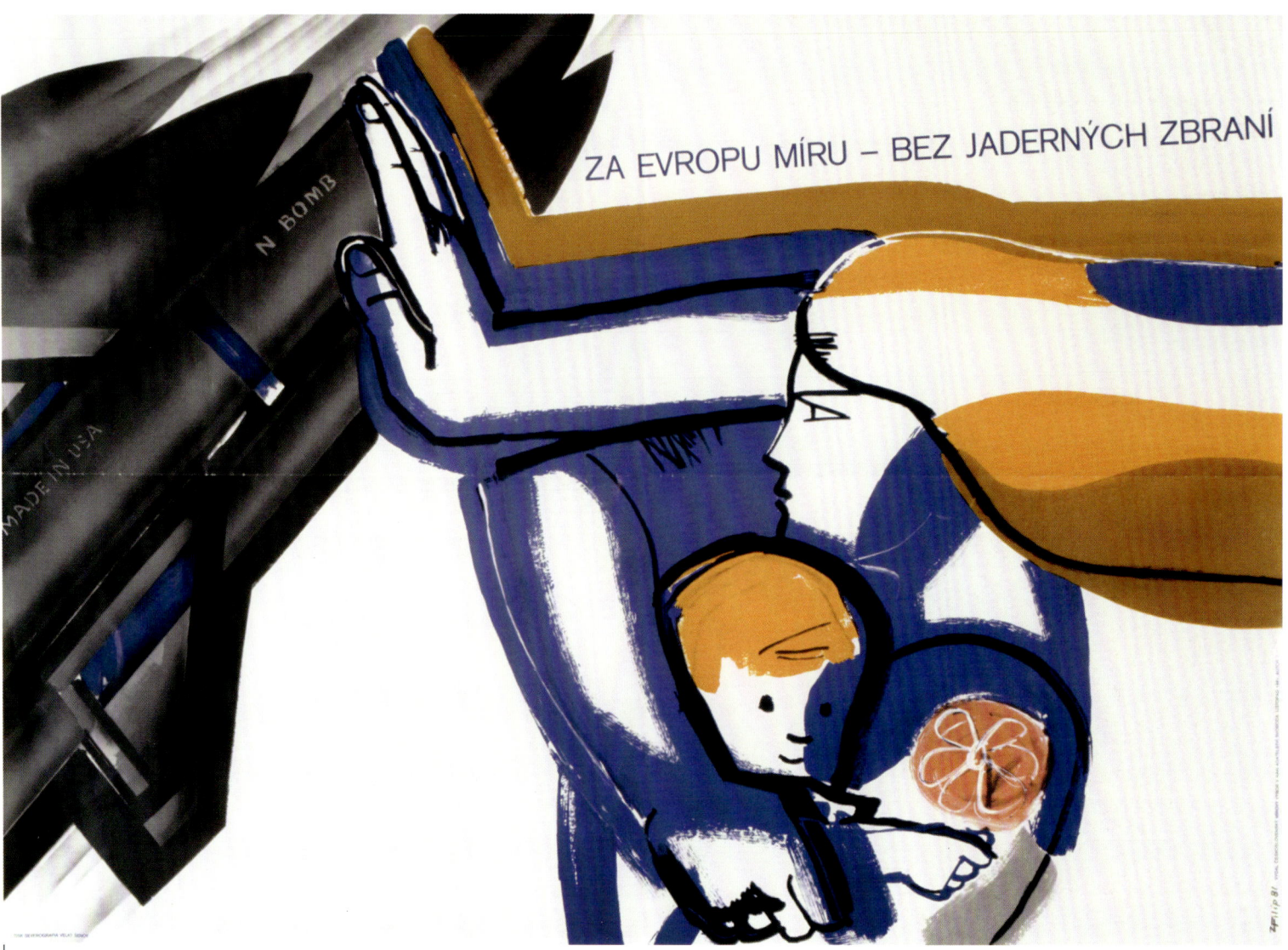

Za evropu míru bez jaderných zbraní
Z. Filip for the Czechoslovak Peace Committee
1981, Czechoslovakia

A mother holds a small child protectively as she faces a nuclear warhead. The bomb is stamped "Made In USA." Its depiction, sleek and defined, contrasts with the mother and child, who possess a more organic appearance expressed through sweeping strokes of color. The child holds a red flower in its hand (a peace offering), emphasizing the juxtaposition of good against evil. Above the mother, an outstretched arm, presumably belonging to another figure just out of shot, pushes the bomb away. The artist has chosen to focus on the mother and child to heighten the poster's impact, but at the same time imply a sense of solidarity and strength in numbers. The text reads: "For a peaceful Europe without nuclear weapons."
It was distributed by the Czechoslovak Peace Committee. Its professed peaceful message masks underlying communist-bloc propaganda and highlights the increased tension between the Soviet Union and the US, where President Reagan had just come to office, switching from a policy of "detente" to one of "rollback."

Pax Sovietica
Polish Solidarity Movement Poster
1982, Poland

The artist of this poster is unknown and it was printed secretly on an underground press. Its simple design depicts a dove, with an olive branch held in its beak—a universal symbol of peace—as a tank, conjured by its continuous-track wheels and armored plate flanks. Two words, "Pax Sovietica" (Soviet Peace), appear at the bottom. Although simple in design, the message conveyed is compelling and seeks to reveal the reality of communist rule. The ostensible Soviet pursuit of peace through organizations such as the Soviet Peace Committee masked the truth that many people living under Soviet control faced a tough life, and any criticism or deviation from communist ideology was dealt with harshly. On December 13, 1981, communist authorities declared martial law in Poland in order to stop the prodemocracy-driven Solidarity trade union (see page 119 for more) from growing in popularity. Martial law was lifted on July 22, 1983, but many activists who had been imprisoned were not released until 1986. The Polish government justified the heavy-handed approach by stressing the threat of Soviet military intervention.

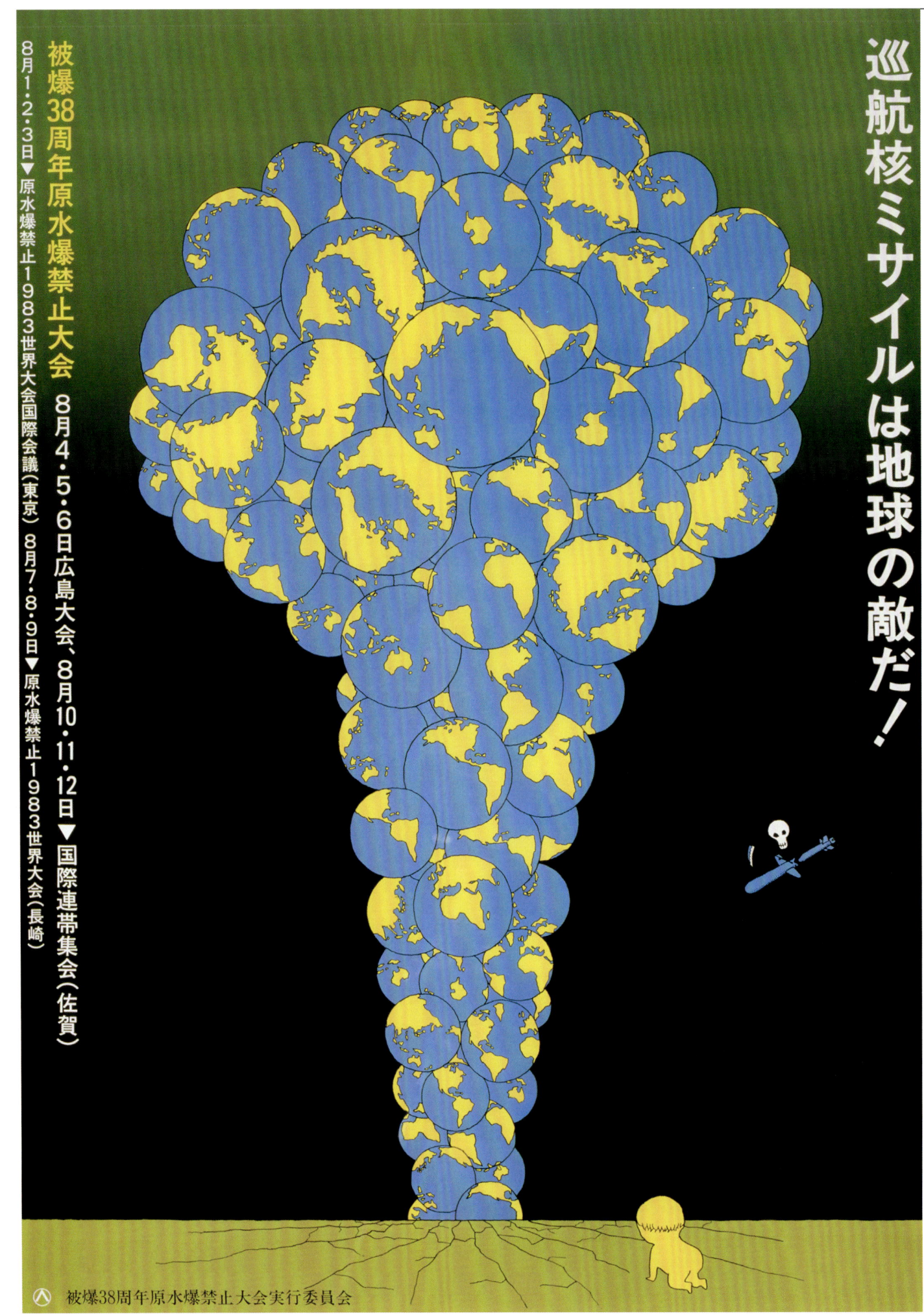

Japanese peace campaign poster during the cold war
Artist unknown, The Japan Council against Atomic and Hydrogen Bombs (Gensuikyo)
1983, Japan

This 1983 Japanese peace poster was produced in response to the threat of nuclear war during the Cold War. On the right the text reads "Cruise nuclear missiles are the enemy of the earth" with dates for a series of antinuclear conferences being held across Japan by Gensuikyo on the left. From a cracked surface, a collection of globes ascends to form the shape of a mushroom cloud. In the foreground, a baby crawls towards this cluster of colliding worlds that are quite literally going up in smoke. To the right, a skull hovers over a nuclear missile, an ever-present threat lurking on the horizon. The background of the poster graduates from murky green at the top to black at the bottom. This period in history saw a deterioration in the relationship between the Soviet Union and the West, following the Soviet invasion of Afghanistan and the huge increases in arms spending by the United States.

Untitled poster
Drawing in 1975 by Kazuo Akiyama
1983, Germany

The poster reads: "Hiroshima teaches: We cannot help you. Doctors, nurses, carers warn against nuclear war!" Below these words there is a drawing of a dying mother trying to shield her two children from the effects of the atomic bomb dropped on Hiroshima in 1945. The original drawing was in color, but this stark depiction in black and white adds to the sense of despair, and the simple line drawing evokes a primal connection that makes the sense of hopelessness palpable. The original drawing by Kazuo Akiyama is held in the Hiroshima Peace Memorial Museum in Japan and includes details of the subject's death; the mother was 1,300 metres from the hypocenter of the bomb, near Tenma-cho. She tried to flee but fell to the ground and burned up trying to protect her two children. The poster goes on to say that, according to the World Health Organization, in a nuclear war, it is virtually impossible to provide medical aid.

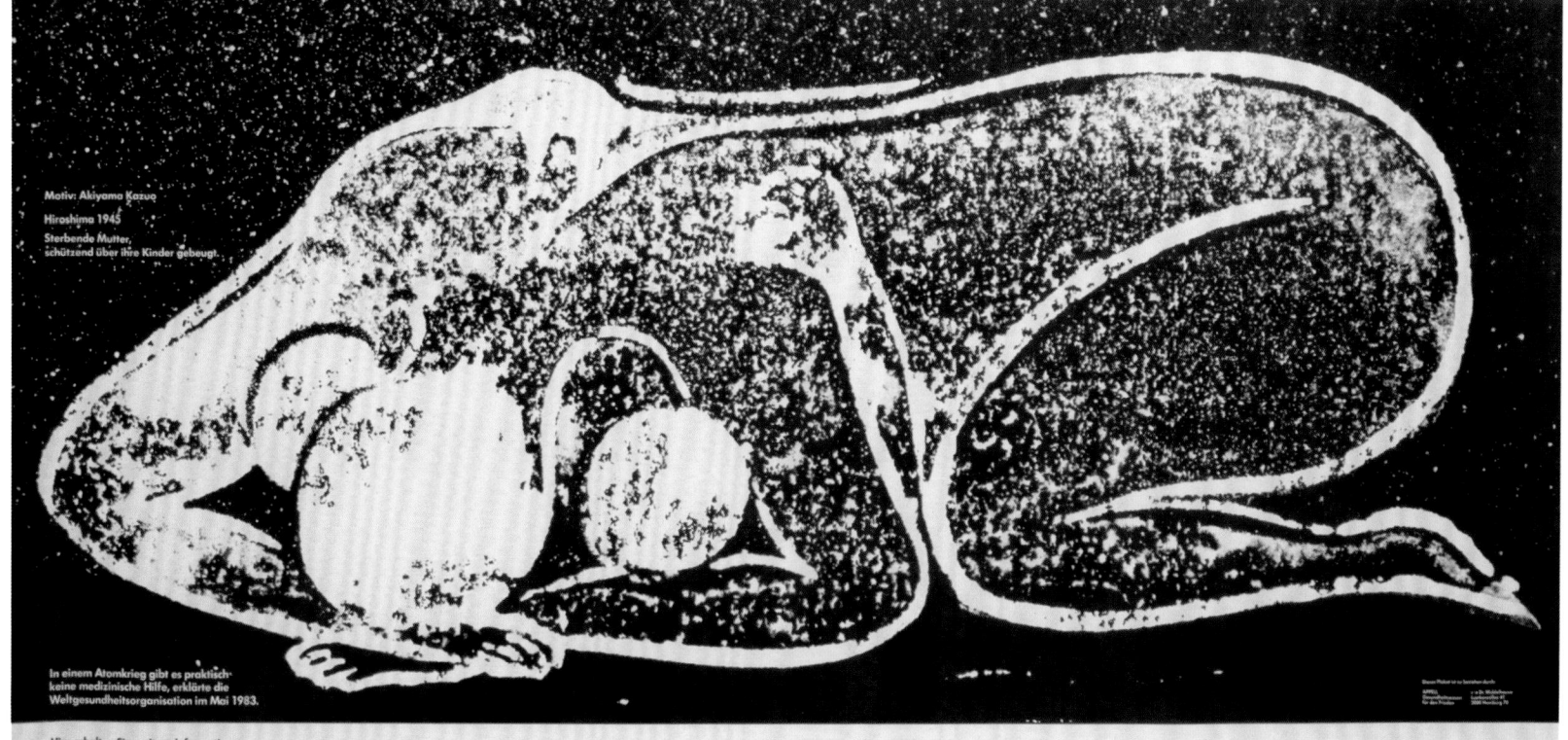

**Stand Together
Easter 1983**
Campaign for Nuclear Disarmament (CND)
1983, UK

Following the Second World War, there was a growing concern about nuclear weapons. The Campaign for Nuclear Disarmament (CND), an organization whose logo has come to be recognized as the international symbol of peace, began in England in 1958. It hit peak popularity during the 1980s, when it was arguably the world's largest peace movement. This poster from 1983 calls for people to "build a living chain to break the nuclear chain!" and shows a "peace-chain" of paper-doll-like cutouts. Their imperfectness suggests they have been crafted by a child's hand. The patterned background of blue and green bands appears to be knitted and adds to the homespun, hand-made feel, in contrast to the hard, cold reality of nuclear war. On April 1, 1983, a chain of tens of thousands of people stretched for more than twelve miles along what protestors referred to as the "nuclear valley": the three places named on the poster—from the American airbase at Greenham Common, via the nuclear research centre at Aldermaston to Burghfield in Berkshire, southern England, the site of a nuclear weapons assembly factory.

Make Tea Not War
Dave Buonaguidi for Karmarama,
Photo by David H. Ramsey
2003, UK

In 2003, Dave Buonaguidi created the now iconic Make Tea Not War poster for an antiwar march held in London, protesting the military invasion of Iraq. It features a collage image of Tony Blair, the then British prime minister, poised with a gun and wearing a teacup on his head. The use of the teacup in place of a soldier's helmet emphasizes the absurdity of war, and plays on the British preoccupation with drinking tea as an almost medicinal activity. The march was organized by the Stop the War Coalition (StWC)—which had formed in opposition to the invasion of Afghanistan in 2001—and took place on February 15, 2003. Large-scale protests were also held in more than 600 cities worldwide. Europe saw the biggest mobilization of protesters, including a rally of three million people in Rome, listed in the *Guinness Book of Records* as the largest ever antiwar rally. Coordinated to occur simultaneously around the world, these 2003 anti-war protests have since been described as "the largest protest event in human history."

Afghanistan Time To Go
David Gentleman for Stop the War Coalition
2006–2011, UK

Designed by British artist David Gentleman, this placard was distributed by the Stop the War Coalition (StWC)—a British group established on September 21, 2001, shortly after the 9/11 attacks, to campaign against the "war on terror." It is one of a series that have been produced over time, and the ubiquitous designs have been seen at numerous antiwar marches in the UK, protesting against the invasions of Afghanistan and Iraq by UK and US armed forces. Believing that, due to the sheer volume of protesters on these marches, something simple but impactful was needed, this placard's prominent word is "GO." (The original in the series said "NO.") The bloodstains were a later addition to help provoke an emotive response. Others in the series have included: "Troops Home," "Bliar" (in reference to UK Prime Minister Tony Blair) and, more recently, "Stop Trident."

> "YOU CAN NO MORE WIN A WAR THAN YOU CAN WIN AN EARTHQUAKE. WAR IS THE SLAUGHTER OF HUMAN BEINGS, TEMPORARILY REGARDED AS ENEMIES, ON AS LARGE A SCALE AS POSSIBLE."
>
> *Jeannette Rankin*
> AMERICAN POLITICIAN, SUFFRAGIST, AND PACIFIST

UNTHINKING RESPECT FOR AUTHORITY IS THE GREATEST ENEMY OF TRUTH

Albert Einstein

GERMAN-BORN THEORETICAL PHYSICIST

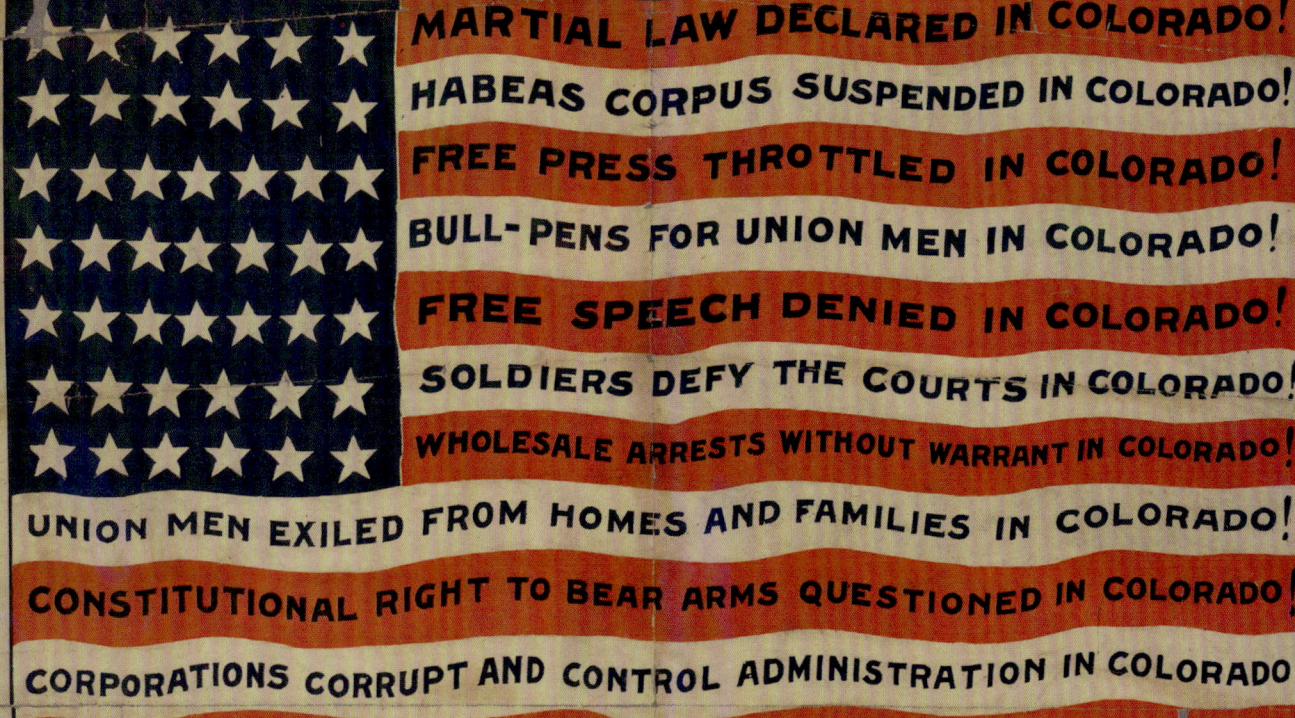

Is Colorado In America?
Western Federation of Miners
c. 1904, USA

This poster with its litany of human rights abuses caused one of its cosigners—president of the Western Federation of Miners (WFM) Charles Moyer—to be arrested on a charge of flag desecration. Signed by Moyer on the bottom left, and by fellow union leader and activist William D. Haywood on the bottom right, the poster was conceived during the Colorado Labor Wars of 1903 and 1904, during which the WFM clashed violently with mine-owners and their government cronies. Colorado governor James Peabody declared martial law and presided over a one-way street of law and order that favored the capitalist mine-owners and saw strikers threatened, evicted from their homes, and arrested as "vagrants." Although arrested, Moyer was never prosecuted, and the event brought home the pertinence of the question raised in the poster: "Is Colorado in America?" Or, what matters most, the flag itself or the values it upholds? The topic remains heated; since the 1989 US Supreme Court ruling that laws banning desecration are themselves unconstitutional, several attempts have been made to introduce a flag desecration law.

Workers of the World Unite!
Dmitry Moor
1931, USSR

Dmitry Moor was the professional moniker of Soviet artist Dmitry Stakhievich Orlov, best known for his political propaganda posters. In this two-paneled poster, the poles of capitalism and socialism are pitted against each other. The "heroic" worker here looms over collected "imperialist" enemies, including the armed figure of fascism and the railing orthodox church. The text on the left reads "against the class of exploiters," while the text on the right calls for the workers of the world to unite. Moor favored the colors black and red, with red reserved solely for socialist elements, such as the workers' badge worn here. Realizing the need for simple communication—the intended audience of peasant workers being largely illiterate—Moor uses simple, bold shapes and a short headline in this poster. In the early part of the twentieth century, unification of workers was seen as integral to revolution and the instigation of a new order.

La Police s'affiche aux Beaux Arts. Les Beaux Arts affichent dans la rue.
Atelier Populaire
1968, France

The events of "Mai '68"—a period of civil unrest in France that threatened the de Gaulle government—started with university students demanding the right to sleep with each other and ended with eleven million workers striking. The baby boom following the Second World War meant there were suddenly more students than ever before, and universities were poorly equipped to handle the numbers, with construction of new buildings slow and teachers hastily trained. At Nanterre University, students clashed with authorities, eventually leading to the closing of the university and threatened expulsion for the "agitators." To show solidarity, Sorbonne students occupied their university courtyard on May 3. Riot police were called in, removing the students and sealing off the university. Protests spread to the streets, an event captured by the slogan on this poster from Atelier Populaire (art students from L'École des Beaux-Arts), which says: "The police are in the art school, the art school is in the street." The government's heavy-handed approach solicited public sympathy for the students, and by the middle of May more strikes had spread to factories, and the crisis had grown to the point where many people demanded the ousting of President de Gaulle.

"A CHANGE IS BROUGHT ABOUT BECAUSE ORDINARY PEOPLE DO EXTRAORDINARY THINGS."

Barack Obama
FIRST AFRICAN AMERICAN US PRESIDENT

Is This The American Way?
Rhode Island School of Design
1968, USA

This screen-printed poster was made by students at the Rhode Island School of Design and was one of a series that were wheat-pasted around campus in protest at the Vietnam War. Although they were colored according to which paint had been donated, the solid black hue of this poster is more than apt. An abridged image of a helmeted soldier wearing a gas mask confronts the viewer. Devoid of any features that might identify it as human, the head is instantly a monstrous and faceless enemy. The subversion of the poster's message—"Is This The American Way?"—highlights the strong and growing opposition to the Vietnam War and the hypocrisy of an ethos that, at home, adheres to the principles of life, liberty, and dignity of the individual, while elsewhere delivering oppression, injustice, and the blackness of death.

Don't Bank On Amerika
Artist unknown. Berkeley Graphic Arts.
1970, USA

In the US, the satiric misspelling "Amerika" was common in left-leaning political material during the sixties and seventies, and served to equate the US government with that of European fascism. The imagery in this one-color poster—a broken dollar sign; a fallen Bank of America sign; and the ruins of a building engulfed in flames from which a truncated forearm thrusts a lit torch—commemorates the burning of the Isla Vista branch of the Bank of America in Santa Barbara, California, on February 25, 1970. Leading up to the event, there had been ongoing tension between students at University of California, Santa Barbara (UCSB) and the police. It came to a head when twenty-two-year-old Rich Underwood was beaten and arrested after leaving an on-campus talk by William Kunstler, lawyer for the Chicago Seven, a group of activists charged by the federal government with conspiracy for their part in anti-Vietnam War demonstrations. Fueled by anger, students set fire to the bank, seeing it as the embodiment of everything they were up against—authority, capitalism, and a deep entrenchment of the status quo.

Strike
Harvey Hacker
1969, USA

The fist seen here is attributed to Harvey Hacker, a student at Harvard's Graduate School of Design (GSD), who set up a print production line to support student strikes at Harvard University in 1969. Used throughout history as a symbol of dissent and solidarity, the clenched fist gave Hacker a tangible image on which to hang the aggrieved on-campus feeling, thereafter tethering him to the unofficial title among Harvard alumni as "the guy who designed the fist." On April 9, 1969, students from the Students for a Democratic Society (SDS) staged a sit-in at Harvard's University Hall. Growing anger at the Vietnam War had galvanized them to action, but their demands reached beyond the antiwar message. In addition to the call to kick the Reserve Officers' Training Corps (ROTC)—a physical reminder of the university's complicity in the war—off campus, the students petitioned for an end to evictions of working-class people from property the university wanted to develop and for the creation of a black studies program.

"NEVER DOUBT THAT A SMALL GROUP OF THOUGHTFUL, COMMITTED CITIZENS CAN CHANGE THE WORLD. INDEED, IT IS THE ONLY THING THAT EVER HAS."

Margaret Mead
CULTURAL ANTHROPOLOGIST AND AUTHOR

Imperialist Machine
Alfredo Rostgaard,
Organization of Solidarity
with the People of Asia,
Africa and Latin America
(OSPAAAL)
c. 1971, Cuba

OSPAAAL's ethos eschews all forms of capitalism, neoliberalism, and globalization and instead seeks social justice and solidarity with, in particular, developing countries. This philosophy is captured in this poster from Cuban designer Alfredo Rostgaard, who, during his tenure as OSPAAL's artistic director from 1966 to 1975, produced a number of psychedelic, pop art-inspired prints with anti-imperialist doctrines. Evocative of the golden years of Cuban poster art with its bold, flat colors and contemporaneous embodiment of the sixties and seventies, this particular work needs no words to convey its message. With a humorous slant, a small, besuited man sits in the mind of the helmeted soldier and, literally as well as metaphorically, steers the demonic-like fighter. Posters produced for OSPAAAL were distributed folded and stapled inside its official publication, *Tricontinental*, providing an effective way of disseminating the group's message internationally.

Boycott Gulf
Boubaker Adjali,
Pan-African Liberation
Committee
1972, USA

This photograph of a young mother, rifle slung over her shoulders and carrying her child in her arms, was taken in Angola by Algerian journalist and filmmaker Boubaker Adjali. Along with the caption—"There are but two sides in a war. She fights on the side of African freedom. Gulf finances the other"—this poster documents the subject of a student standoff at Harvard University in 1972. Gulf Oil was the largest US investor in Portuguese-controlled Angola, and Harvard was Gulf's largest university investor. The Pan-African Liberation Committee (PALC)—all students at Harvard—led a campaign demanding the university divest its 700,000 shares in the oil company as it supported a repressive regime against the Angolan people. When President-elect Derek Bok announced that Harvard would not be divesting, students occupied his office for a week in protest. In response, he sent his assistant to Angola to investigate firsthand. In the same year, Harvard led the formation of the Investor Responsibility Research Center (IRRC), a nonprofit think tank dedicated to gathering information on socially responsible investment.

THE ART OF PROTEST 111

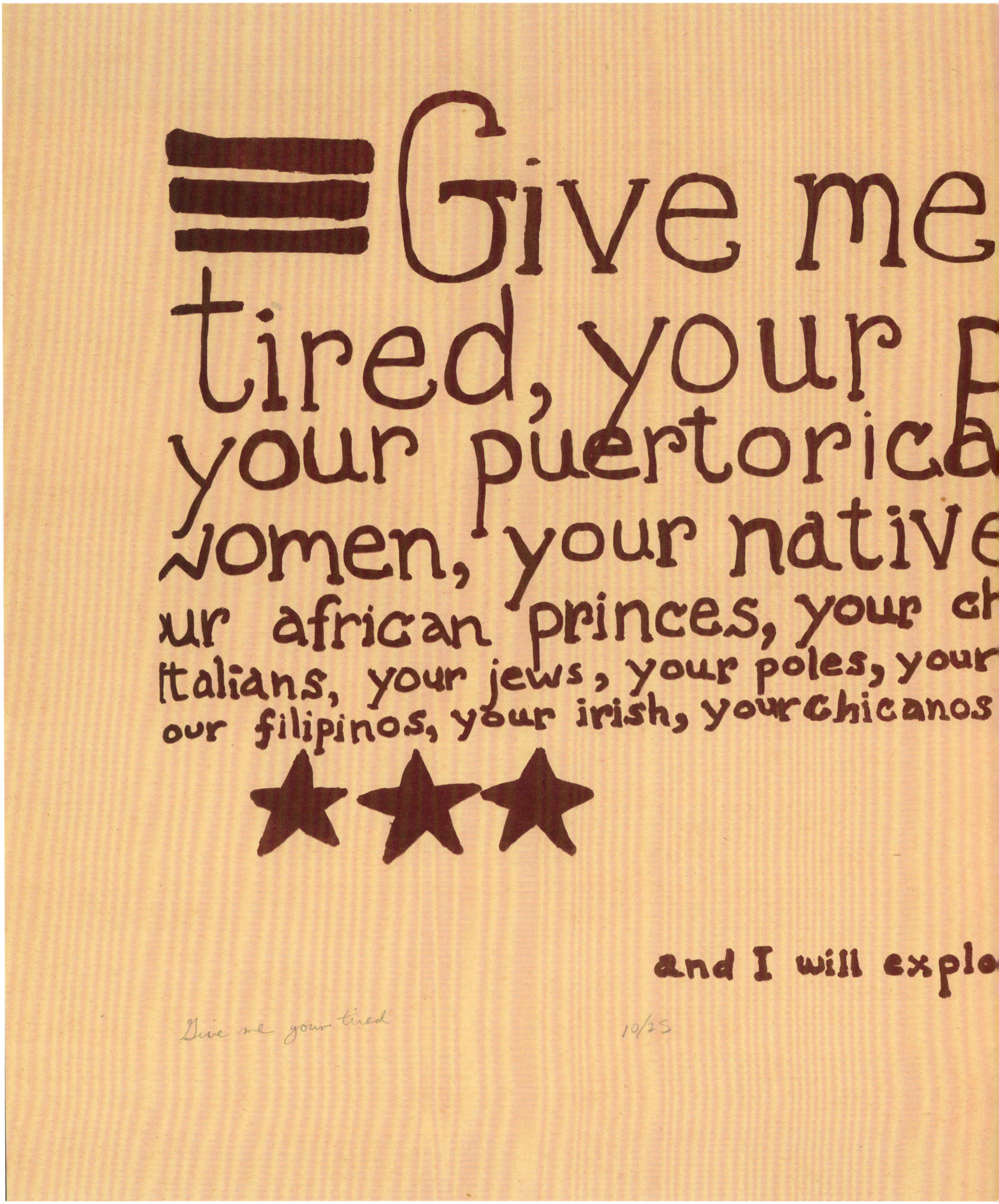

≡ Give me
tired, your p
your puertorica
women, your native
ur african princes, your ch
italians, your jews, your poles, your
our filipinos, your irish, your chicanos

★★★

and I will explo

Give me your tired   10/25

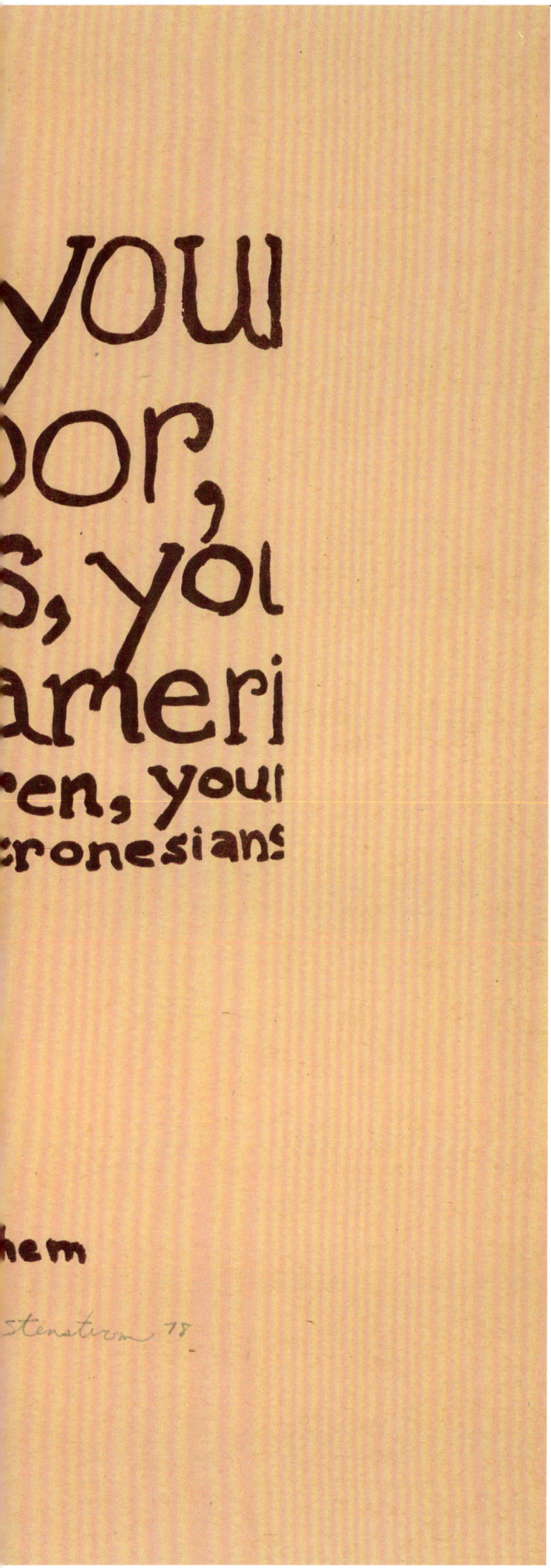

Give me your tired . . . and I will exploit them
Ruth Stenstrom
1978, USA

This poster from American artist Ruth Stenstrom is a riff on "The New Colossus"—the sonnet penned by poet Emma Lazarus in 1883 to raise money for a pedestal for the Statue of Liberty, and which in 1903 was cast onto a bronze plaque and mounted in its lower level. The first two lines on the poster: "Give me your tired, your poor," are from the tenth line of the sonnet; the rest of the text constitutes a list of marginalized, colonized, and subjugated peoples, exploited through the taking of land, denial of rights, and low-wage employment. The script shrinks ever smaller, and the truncated letters on the left and right add to the premise of oppression. "The New Colossus" is often quoted by politicians seeking to reaffirm the US commitment to values of diversity and inclusion, yet this poster stands as a reminder of Liberty's plea to hear the voices of the oppressed.

"EVERY PEOPLE, EVERY SOCIETY, NEEDS A CULTURE OF RESISTANCE, A CULTURE OF BEING DIFFICULT AND DISOBEDIENT, THAT IS THE ONLY WAY THEY WILL EVER BE ABLE TO STAND UP TO THE INEVITABLE ABUSE OF POWER BY WHOEVER RUNS THE STATE APPARATUS, THE CAPITALISTS, THE COMMUNISTS, THE SOCIALISTS, THE GANDHIANS, WHOEVER."

Arundhati Roy
MAN BOOKER PRIZE WINNER AND ACTIVIST

Quelquepart Partout
Alain Le Quernec for Amnesty International
1978, France

This poster was conceived by Alain Le Quernec, a prolific draftsman who took up poster art after seeing its power during the 1968 student revolutions in his home country of France. It is one of many among his portfolio of designs for political and social causes, for which he is well known. A structure shaped from barbed wire and suggestive of a soldier's helmet dangles against a blue sky. A group of people, penned in, can just be seen through the gaps in this particularly brutal enclosure. Suspended amidst a blue abyss and isolated from any visible anchor, the prisoners seem all the more trapped in their confinement. The cagelike cranium also implies a narrative of prisoners of conscience. Together with the poster's text, "Somewhere, everywhere," the image is a stark reminder that people across the globe are imprisoned for little more than their thoughts and ideas.

Boycott!
Comité pour le Boycott des Olympiades de Moscou
1980, France

This poster, produced in support of the boycott of the 1980 Summer Olympics in Moscow, reimagines the Moscow mascot—Misha the bear—as a member of the Russian army. The original mascot, designed by children's book illustrator Victor Chizhikov, was intended to soften the image of the stereotypical big and brutish Russian bear. Although the bear retains his sweetened guise, he is recast in army-issue cap and boots as a Soviet soldier. He has been given a whip to brandish, and barbed wire forms the Olympic rings behind him. The boycott campaign was launched in response to the Soviet invasion of Afghanistan in 1979, and was led by the US. Several countries joined the boycott, with France being one of the first nations to signal their commitment. They did ultimately send athletes to the games, albeit a smaller delegation than originally proposed. The boycott increased tensions between the US and USSR, and Cold War hostilities continued, as the Soviet Union remained in Afghanistan. As payback, the Soviets led a communist bloc counter-boycott of the 1984 Summer Olympics in Los Angeles.

They Cannot Muzzle the Light
Alain Carrier for Amnesty International
1980, France

Prolific poster designer Alain Carrier designed this poster for Amnesty based on a line from the preface of French writer Victor Hugo's *Les Châtiments (Punishments)*—a collection of poems published in 1853 that attack the tyranny of Napoléon III's Second Empire. Featuring a simple line-drawn face masked by coiled barbed wire, the subject's bright-blue eyes stare out at the viewer. The portrait is drawn without a mouth. In its place are the words: "On ne baillonne pas la lumière" (They cannot gag [muzzle] the light), implying that although silenced, a person, the light inside, still speaks. The political landscape against which this poster was designed saw an increased workload for Amnesty in campaigning against torture and on behalf of prisoners of conscience. It faced criticism from several governments, including the USSR, who accused Amnesty of espionage; the Moroccan government, who denounced it as a defender of lawbreakers; and the Argentinian government, who banned publication of Amnesty's 1983 annual report.

Solidarité Mineurs Anglais
Confédération générale du travail (CGT)
c. 1984, France

The sketched face of the coal miner is most likely based on a photograph by Gérald Bloncourt—a Haitian-born artist expelled from his birth country for antigovernment protests in 1946. Bloncourt settled in Paris and dedicated his life to photographing the lives of the Parisian proletariat—immigrants and workers of the suburban shanty towns that had emerged in the city at the end of the Second World War. Bloncourt was also a painter, poet, and writer and a longtime member of the CGT, who distributed this poster. Behind the portrait of the miner, the Tricolour and the Union Jack merge. The poster was produced in support of the British miners' strike of 1984–1985; French coal miners were one of many international communities who gave direct help to the strikers and their families with charitable donations and food convoys. Additionally, the CGT arranged for around two hundred children of the British miners to holiday with French mining families in the Nord-Pas-de-Calais Mining Basin over the summer of 1984.

Haiti

Seit Jahrhunderten
Schreib ich deinen Namen in Sand
Und immer wieder tilgt ihn das Meer
Und immer wieder tilgt ihn der Schmerz
Und jeden Morgen schreib ich ihn wieder
In den tausendjährigen Sand
Meiner Beharrlichkeit

René Depestre

Haiti
René Depestre (words)
Amnesty International
1985, Germany

This poster was designed for Amnesty International Germany to draw attention to human rights abuses in Haiti. Notorious for its lack of democracy, and a place where torture and kidnappings were commonplace, Haiti suffered greatly under the thirty-year dictatorship of the Duvalier family. François Duvalier, known as "Papa Doc," became president in 1957, followed by his son Jean-Claude Duvalier ("Baby Doc") in 1971. During their rule, it is estimated that between 30,000 and 60,000 civilians perished. Rendered in traditional Caribbean colors, the poster depicts a densely packed population ascending Haiti's mountainous landscape. At the bottom, a poem from Haitian writer and activist René Depestre, who was exiled from his birth country in 1946 following his involvement in student protests against the government, reinforces the themes of suffering and persistence. It reads:
"For centuries
I've written your name in sand
And again and again it is erased by the ocean
And again and again it is erased by the pain
And every morning I write it again
Into the thousand-year-old sand
Of my perseverance."

> "IF YOU ARE NEUTRAL IN SITUATIONS OF INJUSTICE, YOU HAVE CHOSEN THE SIDE OF THE OPPRESSOR. IF AN ELEPHANT HAS ITS FOOT ON THE TAIL OF A MOUSE AND YOU SAY THAT YOU ARE NEUTRAL, THE MOUSE WILL NOT APPRECIATE YOUR NEUTRALITY."
>
> *Desmond Tutu*
> SOUTH AFRICAN ANGLICAN CLERIC AND HUMAN RIGHTS ACTIVIST

Solidarność
Tomasz Sarnecki
1989, Poland

In a bid to encourage the people of Poland to vote for the burgeoning Solidarity party founded by Lech Wałęsa in 1980—the first trade union in a Warsaw Pact country not controlled by the Communist Party—this 1989 election poster draws heavily on the country's love of US-style democracy. It features quintessential American cowboy Gary Cooper from the 1952 film *High Noon*. His pistol has been replaced by a ballot paper, and the addition of the solidarity logo pinned above his sheriff's badge equips him for a "high noon" moment—June 4, 1989; election day. Solidarity's logo was conceived by graphic designer Jerzy Janiszewski, who coined a style of writing known as "Solidaric," a joined-up font with the Polish flag flying from the letter "n" to embody a unified country. It was a sentiment endorsed by the electorate when the once-outlawed Solidarity Party swept to success, with Tadeusz Mazowiecki becoming the first noncommunist Polish prime minister since 1946. Lech Wałęsa was later elected in 1990.

Occupy. Liberate. Decolonize.
Slingshot Media, Occupy Berkeley
2011, USA

The worldwide Occupy movement took off in earnest on September 17, 2011, with Occupy Wall Street the first to receive widespread attention. Largely understood as a left-wing, anticapitalist movement, it sparked protests across the globe, and by mid-October there were around nine hundred separate movements. This poster was produced in support of Occupy Berkeley, which began on November 9 on the Berkeley campus of the University of California, lauded by many as the birthplace of modern revolutionary activism and also an area considered the ancestral homeland of the Native American Ohlone Chochenyo people. The words "Occupy" at the top and "Decolonize" at the bottom at first seem disparate. Yet the lightning strike that cuts through the word "Liberate" fuses them, encompassing and equating the historical issue of indigenous colonization by Europeans with that of contemporary corporate exploitation. The organic yet fragmented illustration of the word "Decolonize" is a further nod to the issue of gentrification, which is forcing local people from the area in favor of more affluent developments and commercial greed.

We Stand in Solidarity with Freedom Fighters of Rojava
International Anarchist Federation (IFA)
2015, Worldwide

Rojava (the Democratic Federation of Northern Syria [DFNS] or, since September 2018, the Autonomous Administration of North and East Syria [NES]) is a de facto area in northern Syria not officially recognized by the Syrian government, where the Kurdish population has long been discriminated against by the Ba'athist regime. From the chaos of the Syrian civil war, and while also fending off attacks from Islamic State, a largely Kurdish coalition emerged as a new self-governing entity. Women were at the forefront of this revolution, reflected in this poster, which shows a member of the YPJ, Yekîneyên Parastina Jin or women's protection units. The extreme laws restricting women's freedom instituted by Syria's president, Bashar al-Assad, were superseded by an explicit mandate for the equal rights of women and for public institutions to work toward the elimination of gender discrimination. Given the inclusion of the red-and-black star—an anarcho-syndicalism symbol—this poster is likely conceived by the International Anarchist Federation, an international network that claims to work together for a free society through the abolition of authority, whether economic, political, social, religious, cultural, or sexual.

Protect Kids Not Guns
Micah Bazant for Amplifier
2018, USA

Designed especially for March for Our Lives—a student-led protest campaigning for stricter gun laws following the mass shooting at Marjory Stoneman Douglas High School in Parkland, Florida, on February 14, 2018—this poster combines a striking piece of portraiture art with a powerful message of social justice. The juxtaposition of the beauty of the art with such sobering words projects a salient observation about American society. Centering on a young black protestor with their hands up and wearing a t-shirt emblazoned with the words "Don't Shoot," the popular poster was shared widely on social media. The designer deliberately featured a black protestor, in homage to black youths, who for generations have been actively campaigning in often unacknowledged ways to end gun violence in the US; black youths are ten times more likely to be killed by guns than white youths, but deep-rooted racism means they are rarely seen as innocent victims. On March 24, 2018, up to two million people at more than eight hundred events united to honor the memory of the seventeen students and staff killed at Marjory Stoneman Douglas and to demand urgent action, making March for Our Lives one of America's largest ever protests.

There Are Too Many People In Prison
Josh MacPhee, Justseeds
2016, USA

The US has the biggest prison population in the world and the highest incarceration rate, with a criminal punishment system that disproportionately punishes poor people and people of color. Most states spend more money on prisons than education. Against this framework, in 2016, Justseeds artist Josh Macphee produced a series of four posters, of which this is one, for the Amplifier Foundation. Using a shared color palette of red and blue, and featuring simple statements, the posters force questions about America's penal system. A repeated motif of photo-booth-style portraits of young people fills the background and serves to humanize the faceless issue of mass incarceration and draw attention to what's referred to as the school-to-prison pipeline—students pushed out of school due to overly harsh disciplinary procedures are more likely to be incarcerated. Since 1974, expulsions from school have almost doubled, largely due to zero-tolerance policies that treat misdemeanors, regardless of severity, on an even measure.

HATE IS TOO GREAT A BURDEN TO BEAR. IT INJURES THE HATER MORE THAN IT INJURES THE HATED.

Coretta Scott King

ACTIVIST AND WIFE OF MARTIN LUTHER KING, JR.

Against Apartheid
Ken Sprague for the Boycott Movement
1960, UK

Designed by British political cartoonist and artist Ken Sprague, this poster raises the profile of the Boycott Movement, an activist organization founded in 1959, which eventually became the UK's Anti-Apartheid Movement (AAM). It called for a boycott of South African goods throughout the month of March as a way of peacefully protesting apartheid and was launched on February 28, 1960, at a fifteen-thousand-strong rally held in London's Trafalgar Square. Using a silhouette of a human face viewed in profile, the one-color poster captures the oppositional nature of the oppressive regime and lays bare its racist codes via a simple yet candid approach: the negative space of one face providing the outline of the other, and vice versa. This binary composition was similarly evident in the design of the AAM logo, also conceived by Sprague.

We Shall Overcome. Register–Vote.
Ernest Critchlow
1963, USA

Despite African American men being given the right to vote in 1870 by the Fifteenth Amendment to the Constitution, the reality was that many African American men and women have been excluded from the ballot box by countless devious and ad hoc obstacles laid before them by election officials, from requirements to own property to completing lengthy forms to taking literacy tests. During the civil rights era, the register-vote campaign was central to achieving equality and overcoming disenfranchisement, a sentiment expressed in this poster from 1963, which features an illustration by Ernest Critchlow, an American artist who had emerged from the Works Progress Administration (WPA) Federal Art Project (FAP) and developed a compelling voice on issues affecting African Americans through his social realist style. Holding hands, a mass of people advance towards the viewer. The red-orange print of chain links is broken in half by the words "register-vote." With the heading "we shall overcome," the poster provides a powerful allegorical statement on unity, breaking the chains of oppression, and progress.

THE ART OF PROTEST 127

With Liberty and Justice For All
Frank Cieciorka
1967, USA

This woodcut by veteran civil rights campaigner Frank Cieciorka was described by San Francisco journalist Edward S. Montgomery as "one of the most vile, obscene pieces of literature that I have seen disseminated in San Francisco." Montgomery was testifying before the 1968 House Un-American Activities Committee (HUAC), a congressional committee created in 1938 to scrutinize alleged disloyalty against the state. Eight helmeted policemen are depicted gang-raping the figures of Liberty (to the left, pinned to the ground with her torch still in hand) and Justice (blindfolded in the background and held in a chokehold while the scales of justice languishes in her hand). At the top of the poster, the US emblematic eagle hovers over the scene, which is enclosed at the bottom with the semicircled slogan ". . . With Liberty and Justice for All." In the context of the race riots that spread across the country in the year this print was made, this stark, metaphorical motif holds a mirror to the reality of police violence against African American citizens, the most violent of which took place in Newark, New Jersey and Detroit, Michigan.

Move On Over Or We'll Move Over You
Artist unknown, Lowndes County Freedom Organization (LCFO)
c. 1966, USA

Although featuring a black panther, this is not a Black Panther Party poster. It was issued by the Lowndes County Freedom Organization (LCFO), a grassroots political party in Alabama, founded to increase black voter registration as a means of emancipation from white supremacy. Known as "Bloody Lowndes" because of its violent and entrenched racism, the county had no African American registered voters in 1965—even though the majority of its citizens were black. Stokely Carmichael of the Student Nonviolent Coordinating Committee (SNCC) was charged with correcting that injustice. Frustrated at the futility of registering voters who could only vote for what was essentially a white supremacy party and fueled by the frustrations of the county's repressed African Americans, he helped form a new political party—the LCFO. Literacy rates were low in Alabama, so state law demanded that any political party use a visual symbol. The black panther was a representation of African Americans backed so far into a corner that the only option left is to attack. The symbol created national interest and, in 1966, Huey P. Newton and Bobby Seale asked permission to use it for their newly formed Black Panther Party for Self-Defense.

I Am A Man and Honor King: End Racism
1968, USA

On February 12, 1968, Memphis sanitation workers, the majority of them African American men, went on strike, prompted by the fatalities of two fellow workers who had been crushed to death by a faulty garbage truck. They demanded recognition for their union, better wages, and safer working conditions. They marched bearing posters declaring "I AM A MAN," a poignant plea to be treated as no less than a human being. The strike drew support from Martin Luther King, Jr. On April 3, King delivered his famous "I've Been to the Mountaintop" speech at the Mason Temple in Memphis. It was his last speech. He was assassinated the following night at Memphis's Lorraine Motel. Four days later, his widow, Coretta Scott King, and their children led twenty thousand marchers through the streets of Memphis, holding copies of another poster that read: "Honor King: End Racism!"

Power To The People
Richard Moore
c. 1970, USA

Designed by Richard Moore (who now goes by the name Dhoruba al-Mujahid bin Wahad), this poster protests the incarceration of the Panther 21, a group accused of orchestrating a bombing campaign targeting New York City in 1969, of which bin Wahad was a member. Bin Wahad had acquired his graphics skills as an apprentice at an ad agency and joined the New York chapter of the Black Panthers in 1968 following the assassination of Martin Luther King, Jr. In his poster, a lone figure stands defiantly in front of a row of silhouetted buildings reminiscent of the New York skyline, his raised fist busting out of chains. The slogan "Power to the People" is a reflection of the political atmosphere of the sixties and the growing support that Panther 21 was garnering from the general public, even receiving celebrity support from Leonard Bernstein, who hosted fundraising parties to help raise bail bonds. Members of Panther 21 were acquitted of all charges on May 12, 1971. During the trial, bin Wahad skipped bail and fled to Algeria. He was consequently expelled from the Black Panthers.

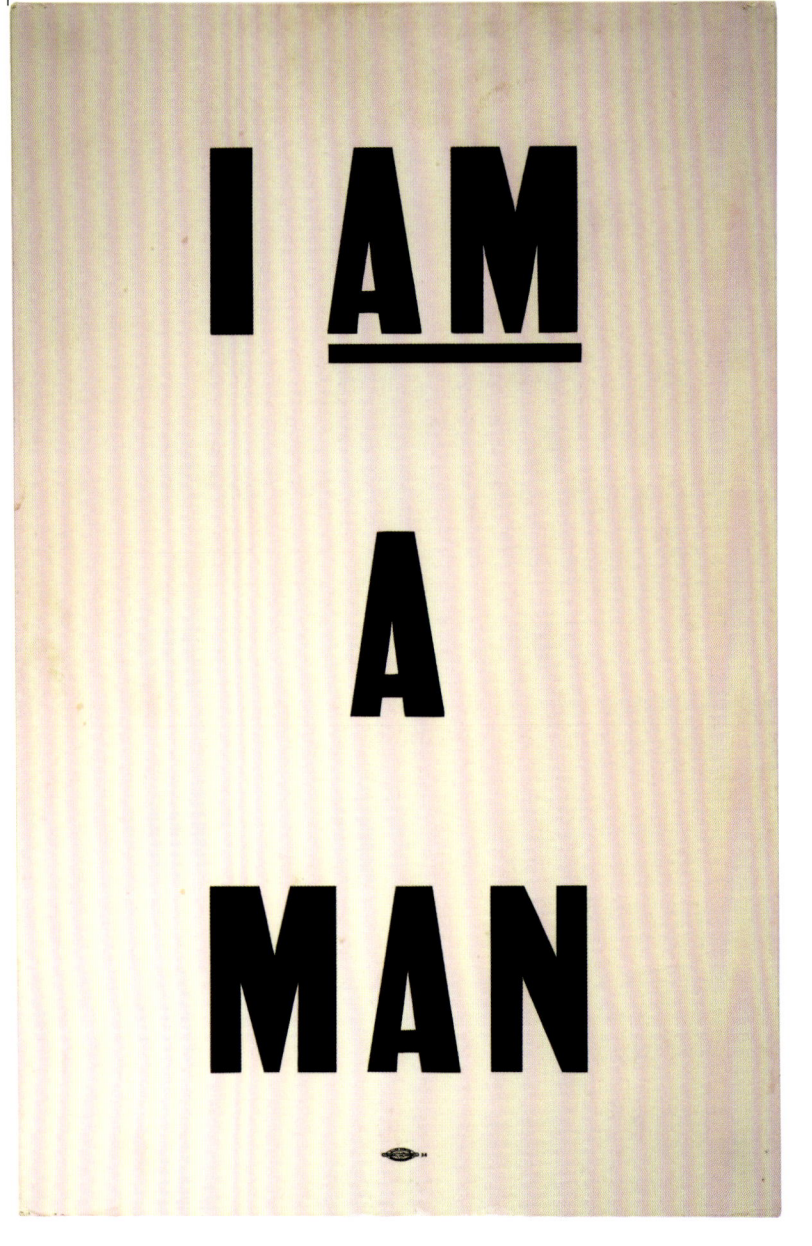

LIBERTAD PARA ANGELA DAVIS

Libertad Para Angela Davis
(Freedom For Angela Davis)
Félix Alberto Beltrán Concepción
1971, USA

Originally designed for the Revolutionary Orientation Department of the Central Committee of the Communist Party in Cuba, this poster was replicated by American organizations, such as this one from the New York Committee to Free Angela Davis. The stylized yet simple design made it easy to copy. Davis was a member of the Communist Party and a vocal supporter of the Black Panther Party. These affiliations ultimately led to her being fired from her teaching post at UCLA, a move directed by then California governor Ronald Reagan. In 1970, she was added to the FBI's Most Wanted list, accused of helping orchestrate the Soledad Brothers' failed escape from Marin County Courthouse, where they were on trial for murdering a prison guard. Based on information that weapons used in the incident were registered to Davis, she was arrested while on the run on October 13, 1970, and charged with kidnapping, murder, and criminal conspiracy. During her imprisonment, a "free Angela" movement lifted her to celebrity status, thanks in part to her instantly recognizable large Afro, which helped propagate her image as synonymous with civil rights activism. Davis was acquitted of all charges on June 4, 1972.

> **"DARKNESS CANNOT DRIVE OUT DARKNESS; ONLY LIGHT CAN DO THAT. HATE CANNOT DRIVE OUT HATE; ONLY LOVE CAN DO THAT."**
> *Martin Luther King, Jr.*
> BAPTIST MINISTER, NOBEL LAUREATE, AND CIVIL RIGHTS LEADER

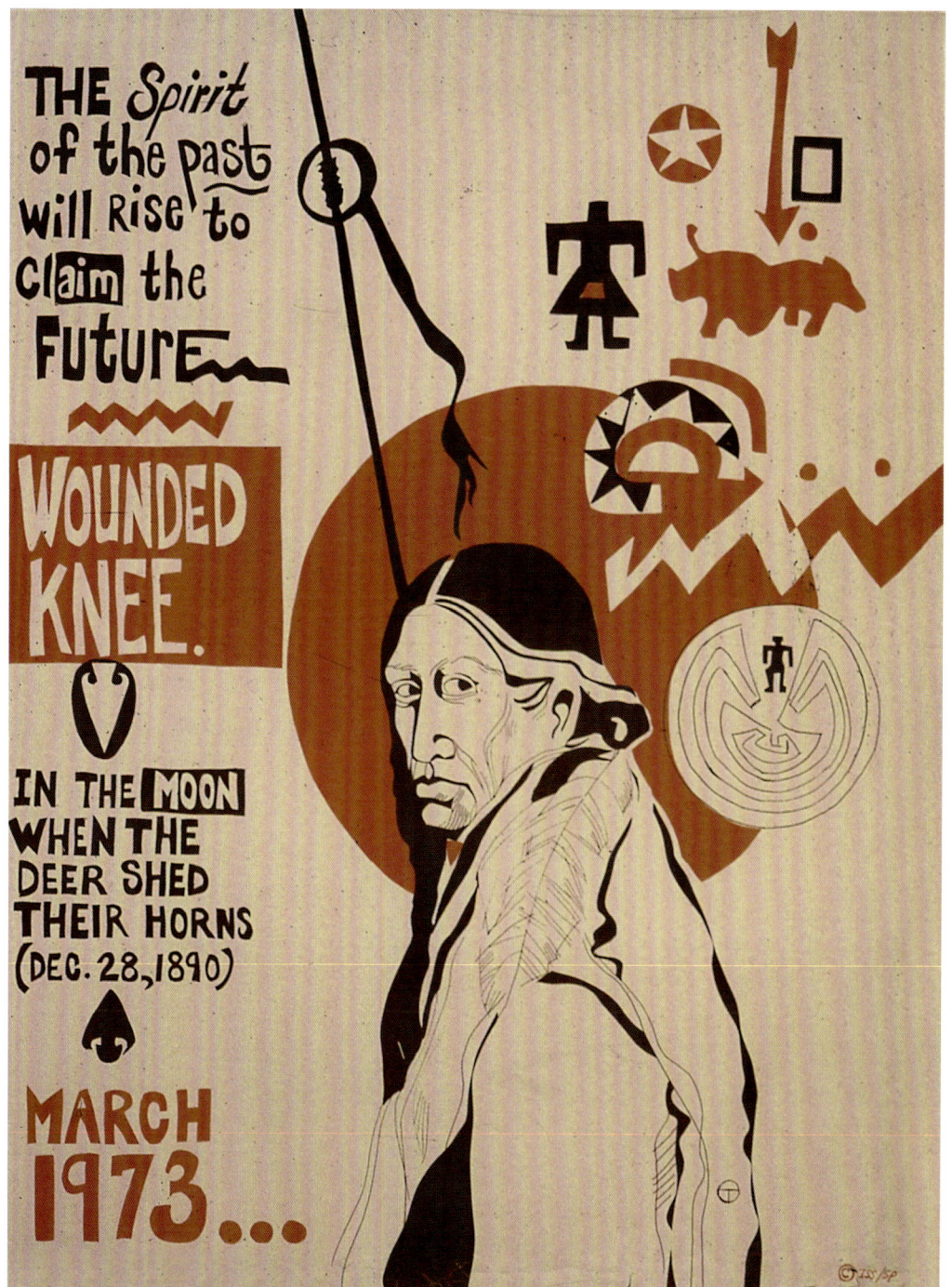

Remember Wounded Knee
Artist unknown
1973, USA

Powerful themes of rebirth and renewal permeate this poster, which commemorates the massacre at Wounded Knee. The predominant color, red, is symbolic in Native American art of new beginnings, and the man-in-the-maze symbol to the right of the hand-drawn portrait represents life and its path, ultimately leading to the next world. Other symbols, such as the downward-pointing arrow denoting peace, and arrowheads signaling alertness, add to the story. In 1890, having lost much of their land, the Lakota Sioux embraced the Ghost Dance, a spiritual dance that promised restoration of peace and prosperity. The US government misinterpreted the dance as a sign of an imminent uprising and launched an attack that claimed between 150 to 300 Sioux (including women and children) and 31 US soldiers. At the time, the general public hailed the soldiers as heroes. Almost a hundred years later, in 1973, the American Indian Movement (AIM) chose the town of Wounded Knee as the site of a 71-day occupation in protest at, among other things, the government's persistent failure to honor treaties with Native American nations. Amid increasing awareness of historic injustices, the protest received public support.

Respect Our Vision . . .
Menominee Solidarity Committee
1975, USA

This reportage-style protest poster tells the story of the Menominee warriors' 1975 occupation of the Alexian Brothers' Novitiate in Gresham, Wisconsin. The photograph shows a lone female wrapped in the American flag. Behind her stand members of the National Guard dressed in riot gear. She is perhaps just keeping warm (the occupation took place during winter), but the image projects the greater symbolic significance of the isolation of the Menominee tribe following their termination from federal control in 1954. Termination sought to abolish the Menominee's status as a sovereign nation with the promise of economic emancipation and hopes of assimilation with mainstream society. In reality, many tribal resources were lost to corporate development, and the Menominee fell quickly into poverty. Although they successfully campaigned for restoration of sovereignty, granted by President Nixon in 1973, for many the process was too slow. The Menominee Warrior Society, in a bid to hasten events, seized the novitiate, occupying it for thirty-four days with demands to turn the land over to the adjacent Menominee Indian Reservation.

Votre Banque Finance L'Apartheid. Halte!
Campagne: 100,000 français contre le financement de l'apartheid
1975–80s, France

Along with the UK and the US, France was one of the largest economic partners of the tyrannical apartheid regime in South Africa. French banks in particular provided a large part of the investment, promoting a reputable front for dirty arms deals. Investment in South Africa was attractive for many foreign partners because of the unique combination of prosperous white customers and cheap black labor. This poster reads "Your Bank Is Financing Apartheid. Stop it!" and shows the anguished face of a young African boy squeezed by the jaws of a checkbook. The image of the child originated from a photograph of a boy playing among other children; his expression of joy was modified to one of pain by Rob van der Aa, a designer from the Dutch boycott campaign Outspan. In France, the Mouvement Anti-Apartheid (MAA), founded in 1975, provided a platform for campaigns with a common aim of isolating the racist regime socially, culturally, and economically. It was largely economic sanctions that brought South Africa to its knees: "The straw which broke the camel's back was the economy. We couldn't afford apartheid any more," admitted Pik Botha.

Free Nelson Mandela And All South African Political Prisoners
Rupert García for the Liberation Support Movement
1981, USA

That Nelson Mandela became the face of the global campaign against apartheid is all the more remarkable given that no one really knew what he looked like. At the time this poster was produced, Mandela had been imprisoned for almost twenty years. Distribution of his image was banned within South Africa, carrying severe penalties such as torture and imprisonment, so many posters were based on an artist's impression, as is the case here. Presented in rich colors, Mandela's face dominates this poster from leading Chicano artist Rupert García, whose work is known for its political stance and bold graphics. Depicted looking directly at the viewer, the image of Mandela is complemented by a direct plea in English for his, and other South African political prisoners', release, with translations in French and Spanish running vertically on the right-hand side. Despite the lack of an accurate portrait of Mandela being readily available, the Free Nelson Mandela campaign became one of the most effective global movements of the twentieth century.

> **"FOR TO BE FREE IS NOT MERELY TO CAST OFF ONE'S CHAINS, BUT TO LIVE IN A WAY THAT RESPECTS AND ENHANCES THE FREEDOM OF OTHERS."**
>
> *Nelson Mandela*
> FORMER PRESIDENT OF SOUTH AFRICA AND ANTI-APARTHEID ACTIVIST

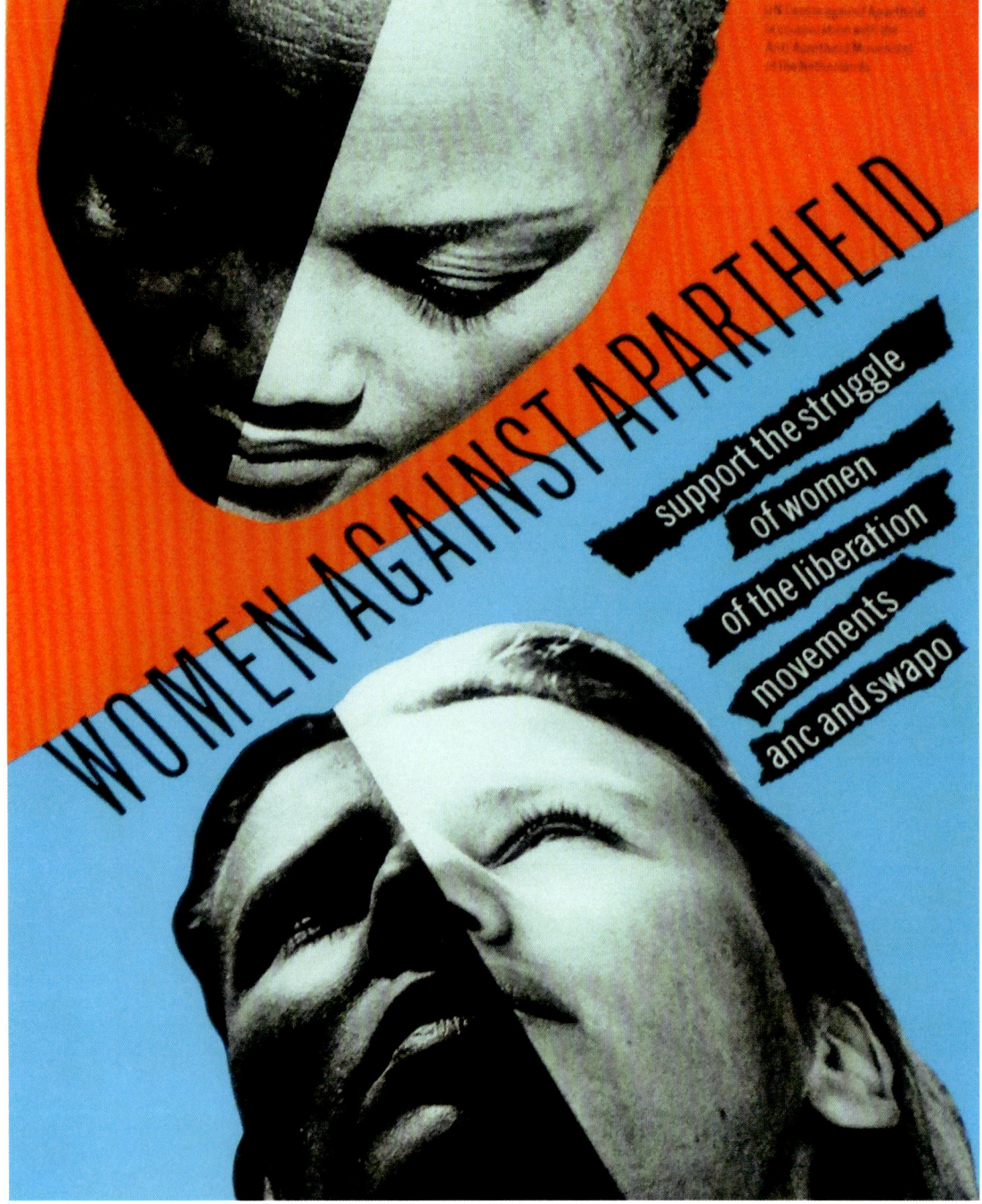

End Apartheid. South Africa Must Be Free. Divest Now
Lincoln Cushing
Inkworks Press
1985, USA

In this poster by artist and archivist Lincoln Cushing, an image of a black male figure, seemingly escaping from the southern tip of Africa, captures the attention of the viewer. A list of American companies with large economic involvement in South Africa is printed in the background. The text—"South Africa Must Be Free. Divest Now"—is a call for the US to withdraw its heavy investment in South Africa and wield its power and influence to challenge the apartheid system rather than prop it up. Companies indicted in the gray background text include major oil companies and banks, who despite public pressure continued to finance the oppressive apartheid regime. The US was one of the biggest investors in Africa, justifying its actions by claiming that American financing provided employment for the black population and therefore improved their standard of living, when in reality it was a system that exploited cheap labor for the benefit of the white minority. The poster was published by Inkworks, a worker-run community print shop that grew out of the Berkley-based activism of the sixties and seventies in northern California.

Women Against Apartheid
Lies Ros, Frank Beekers, and Rob Schröder of Wild Plakken for Anti-Apartheids Beweging Nederland (AABN)
1984, Netherlands

Wild Plakken was a Dutch design group formed in 1977 by former classmates from the Gerrit Rietveld Academie in Amsterdam. Its name means "wild pasting" and refers to the way the group pasted posters around Amsterdam illegally—Schröder was arrested several times—to bring attention to the political and social struggles of the time. Collective working was central to their operation, as was the belief that design should reflect the nature and content of the subject. The group favored collage, specifically photomontage, with juxtaposed images and bold, colorful shapes. The poster here specifically highlights the struggle under apartheid of women, who were subject not only to racial oppression, but also gender discrimination. Two female heads, each with a dark and a light-skinned half, exhibit the conflict of the apartheid system, while the text, "women against apartheid," overlapping the blue and red represents the ultimate aim of unification.

End Apartheid

South Africa Must Be Free Divest Now

State of Terror
Michael Callaghan for Amnesty International Australia
1986, Australia

Designed in response to human rights violations in South Africa, this poster delivers a roll call of civilians disappeared, tortured, or killed while detained by the might of apartheid forces. The design is characteristic of artist Michael Callaghan's idiosyncratic style, using fluorescent blue, red, and yellow inks on a black background, and bold outlines. In addition to names, the poster includes visuals of objects that helped prop up apartheid tyranny, such as gold and diamonds, which frame the depictions of death and torture within. At the time of production, South Africa was living through a national state of emergency, extreme force justified by apartheid rulers in the name of public safety. Under President P. W. Botha, the state of emergency became a normalized part of governance and allowed violent repression against any sign of dissent. The poster was printed by Redback Graphix, an alternative print and design studio founded by Callaghan in 1979 with the aim of supporting political activism. To the bottom right of the figure tied to a chair is the group's signature spider in a red triangle.

You Are On Aboriginal Land
Marie McMahon
1984, Australia

This 1984 poster melds two memories from its artist, Marie McMahon, to protest the grabbing of Aboriginal land in Australia. The depiction of the woman in the print is based on a photograph of Tiwi woman Phillipa Pupangamirri taken by McMahon when she visited Bathurst Island—one of the Tiwi Islands north of Darwin—in 1980. The sentiment derives from a recollection the artist has of another Tiwi woman, Piparo (Winnie Munkara), who confronted Darwinian businessmen scoping out land for a potential tourist development on Bathurst Island, telling them "Tikilaru is not your country." The poster's slogan was borrowed from bumper stickers McMahon had seen in Townsville: "Pay the rent—you are on Aboriginal land." The poster had initially included "Pay the rent," but McMahon later dropped it feeling that it didn't accurately reflect the people she was portraying, or the language they would use.

> "HATING PEOPLE BECAUSE OF THEIR COLOR IS WRONG. AND IT DOESN'T MATTER WHICH COLOR DOES THE HATING. IT'S JUST PLAIN WRONG."
>
> *Muhammad Ali*
> BOXING CHAMPION AND PHILANTHROPIST

End Israeli Apartheid
Josh MacPhee, Justseeds, for the Coalition Against Israeli Apartheid (CAIA)
2006, USA and Canada

An armored bulldozer overlaid with criss-crossing twines of barbed wire compose the chief elements of this poster, produced for the Coalition Against Israeli Apartheid (CAIA) in Montreal, Canada. This type of bulldozer is used by the Israeli Defense Forces (IDF) in Jerusalem, the West Bank, and the Gaza Strip to destroy Palestinian structures, including homes, while barbed wire is a common sight along barriers between Israel and Palestine. Both are seen as a necessary security measure by the Israeli government, but as instruments of oppression and division by many Palestinians and human rights organizations, such as Amnesty International and the United Nations. In 2005, more than 170 Palestinian organizations called for an international campaign of boycott, divestment, and sanctions against Israel.

Stop Racism! Stop Police Violence!
Scott Braley for Fireworks Graphics
1993, USA

The compositional elements of this poster draw together almost thirty years of a pervasive issue, the reality of police brutality and racism. A line from Malcolm X's "Ballot or Bullet" speech from 1964 tops this stark, one-color poster, below which are three silhouetted forms—two police officers looming over a prone figure on the ground. The image refers to the Los Angeles Police Department's (LAPD's) violent beating of Rodney King on March 3, 1991, an incident that ultimately sparked the 1992 Los Angeles riots. Unbeknownst to the four LAPD officers involved, and to King, the predawn events had been captured by civilian George Holliday, who filmed it on his camcorder, and this video—broadcast widely on TV networks—was used to bring the police officers to trial. They were acquitted on April 29, 1992. The injustice of the verdict sparked outrage among African Americans and an uprising that lasted six days. During that period, sixty-three people were killed and more than two thousand injured. The poster was distributed under the Fireworks Graphics Collective—a Bay Area print shop in California operational from 1972 to 1997.

NO JUSTICE
NO PEACE

SUPPORT INDIGENOUS RESISTANCE

No Justice, No Peace
Jesse Purcell, Justseeds, for Idle No More
2012, Canada

Designed in support of the Idle No More movement—one of the largest indigenous movements in Canadian history—this poster calls on people to "support indigenous resistance." The image shows a red hand, its protruding middle finger sheathed with Canada's iconic Peace Tower, which sits atop Canadian parliamentary buildings in Ottawa. Used here, it highlights the hypocrisy of passing laws that violate the peace and human rights of Canada's First Nation communities. Canada is one of the world's wealthiest nations. Its riches, Idle No More claim, were made by plundering First Nations' land of resources through mining, logging, and fishing, threatening not only their sovereignty but also the environment. The Idle No More movement exists to address these injustices in order to foster peace between indigenous communities and settler societies.

Black Lives Matter (BLM)
Josh Warren-White for Design Action Collective
2013, USA

Since its inception in 2013, Black Lives Matter has grown from a hashtag coined by three black community organizers—Alicia Garza, Patrisse Cullors, and Opal Tometi—to a global social justice movement. Following the acquittal of neighborhood watch coordinator George Zimmerman for the murder of African American teen Trayvon Martin, Garza penned a love letter to black people, which she shared on Facebook. It included the line, "Our Lives Matter, Black Lives Matter." Cullors and Tometi added their support and #BlackLivesMatter launched across social media. The emerging movement needed a pictorial embodiment, so the three women enlisted Design Action Collective to help conceive a logo. The initial brief was for an easily replicable design for use on their Tumblr page only. Taking the form of a simple wordmark using the Anton font, the all-caps letters rendered in black on a yellow background resulted in a strong and clearly identifiable emblem. Designer Josh Warren-White explained: "We wanted to make something that people could pick up and use in myriad ways." Such was its success that the logo has since been co-opted by corporate and community bodies alike, which some feel dilutes BLM's original message about racial injustice.

We are using resources as if we had two planets, not one. There can be no "Plan B" because there is no "Planet B."

Ban Ki-moon

FORMER SECRETARY-GENERAL OF THE UNITED NATIONS

Untitled poster
Hans Rudi Erdt for Gesellschaft fuer rauchfreien Autobetrieb (GRA)
1910, Germany

Germany has been widely seen as the home of the modern-day car. In much the same way, this poster is an example of a modern style of poster art that emerged in Germany at the beginning of the twentieth century. Rejecting the complexities of Art Nouveau, the poster's composition consists of streamlined drawings rendered in flat colors. The style was known as "Sachplakat," or "Plakatstil," of which this poster's artist, Hans Rudi Erdt, was a key proponent. The poster was published by Hollerbaum & Schmidt, a leading poster printing company in Berlin, and advocates for environmentally friendly, low-emission cars.

Protect Your Parks
Stanley Thomas Clough for the Federal Art Project (FAP)
1938, USA

Ohio-born Stanley Thomas Clough was one of around ten thousand artists supported by the Federal Art Project (FAP)—a New Deal arts program that employed out-of-work artists during the Great Depression. The program produced more than twenty thousand individual works of art, from large-scale murals in civic buildings to smaller works such as this screen-printed poster. President Franklin D. Roosevelt was a keen conservationist, and during his term in office he invested heavily in expanding the country's network of parks and forests. His influence brought record numbers of people to America's parks and open spaces, and his legacy forged national interest in their protection. In his words, "There is nothing so American as our national parks."

Earth Day
Robert Rauschenberg
1970, USA

Earth Day was the idea of Wisconsin senator Gaylord Nelson after he witnessed the devastating effects of an oil spill off the coast of Santa Barbara, California. Launched in 1970, it was initially pitched as a national teach-in across schools and universities in America to raise awareness of environmental issues. During the sixties and seventies a new consciousness about the environment emerged— a burgeoning, collective social awareness that demanded change. Earth Day 1970 is largely acknowledged as the start of the modern environmental movement, leading to the creation of the Environmental Protection Agency (EPA) and the passing of the Clean Air, Clean Water, and Endangered Species acts. Earth Day went global in 1990 and is now honored annually on April 22. Seen here is the first Earth Day poster, designed by American artist and committed environmentalist Robert Rauschenberg. A series of black-and-white images portraying the planet's decay—from endangered animals, such as the gorilla, to polluted cities and barren landscapes—surround an image of the national emblem, the bald eagle, itself, at the time, at risk of extinction.

Freedom to Breathe
Carl F. Meyers, Jr. for United States Public Health, Education and Welfare
1969, USA

Reminiscent of rock posters of its time, this artwork features the Statue of Liberty—America's best-known symbol of freedom—wearing a gas mask to illustrate the country's need to address air pollution. The swirling Art Nouveau-esque text reads: "Freedom to Breathe. Control Air Pollution." In adopting this psychedelic aesthetic, the US government appealed directly to young, postwar baby boomers, many of whom were seeking alternative, more socially aware lifestyles to those of their parents. The poster was distributed a year before the first Earth Day in 1970 and originally included a blank white space along the bottom for people to write their own words of solidarity.

> **"THE EARTH IS WHAT WE ALL HAVE IN COMMON."**
> *Wendell Berry*
> WRITER AND ENVIRONMENTAL ACTIVIST

A wonderful bird is the pelican;
His mouth holds more than his bellican,
He takes in his beak,
Enough food for a week,
But I'm damned if I see how the hellican.

The next pelican you see may be the last one you will ever see.

Join the fight to ban the DDT type pesticides which threaten extinction.

INFORM YOURSELF

A Wonderful Bird Is The Pelican
Berkeley Graphic Arts
c. 1970, USA

Using an ink drawing of a pelican and an oft-cited limerick from American poet and humorist Dixon Lanier Merritt, this poster opposes the use of the chemical Dichlorodiphenyltrichloroethane, or DDT. Originally hailed as a wonder drug in the control of malaria and typhus during the Second World War, DDT went on to be used extensively as a pesticide. By 1948, it was available for public sale in the US. By 1970, the brown pelican was recognized by the US Fish and Wildlife Service as an endangered species. Opposition to DDT stemmed from the seminal 1962 book *Silent Spring*, in which author Rachel Carson analyzed the chemical's devastating effect on wildlife, in particular birds. Public resistance to the use of DDT grew and eventually led to a ban in 1972. The poster was printed by Berkeley Graphic Arts (1967-1971), a printing press borne out of the University of California at Berkeley's Free Speech Movement Press, which had grown (and been renamed twice over) from its original cause of on-campus concerns to capture wider social issues such as the environment, civil rights, and the antiwar movement.

Non a l'Autoroute Rive Gauche (No to the Left Bank Highway)
Raymond Savignac
c. 1972, France

Protesting the construction of a motorway on the Left Bank in Paris, this poster shows a historic building (possibly the Notre-Dame de Paris) personified, waving its arms as if drowning in a sea of cars. It was designed by Raymond Savignac, a French graphic designer best known for his commercial posters done in a simple, humorous style. This poster is in keeping with that simple style, yet the drawing is almost completely monotone, in stark contrast to Savignac's usual, colorful compositions, which accentuates the gravity of the situation. Paris is a severely congested city notorious for traffic jams. In the early 1970s, Prime Minister Georges Pompidou embarked on a program of modernization for Paris, including the expansion of roads. He was an avid motorist, famously saying, "The French love their cars."

THE ART OF PROTEST 153

The Dirty Dozen
Environmental Action, Inc.
1974, USA

The "Dirty Dozen" campaign was an effective way of exposing congressional members who consistently voted against environmental issues, holding them accountable to their consciences and encouraging voter education. This poster was distributed by Environmental Action, a young activist group that grew out of the buzz surrounding the 1970 Earth Day organization and remained operational until 1996. Drawing data from the League of Conservation Voters, an advocacy group that, also in 1970, started to track the voting records of members of Congress on environmental issues, the poster features the faces of twelve members of Congress—Democrats and Republicans—superimposed onto a sketch of a sports team from the early twentieth century. Each has a "D" on their sweater for "Dirty Dozen," in reference to their antigreen voting records.

"THANK GOD MEN CANNOT FLY, AND LAY WASTE THE SKY AS WELL AS THE EARTH."
Henry David Thoreau
POET, PHILOSOPHER, AND ABOLITIONIST

**Nuclear Wastes Make Us Atomic Slaves
Generation After Generation**
Hard Rain
c. 1977, USA

The atomic whirl forms the focus of this poster. Inside the nucleus, the spiraling text reads: "Plutonium remains deadly for thousands of years." Three embryonic illustrations and three human figures bound in chains surround the spiral against a backdrop of the repeated slogan: "Generation After Generation." The poster was produced by a Boston-based protest group, Hard Rain, who had joined the growing opposition to the construction of a nuclear power plant at Seabrook, New Hampshire. Favoring a more militant approach than the majority protest group Clamshell Alliance—which had steadily built support by staging sit-ins at the site, the largest of which drew more than two thousand protestors—Hard Rain argued that anarchistic tactics such as fence-cutting would help attract larger numbers of working-class people to the cause. Of the two reactors planned at Seabrook, only one was ever built.

"Dumb Animals"
Greenpeace. Photography by David Bailey
1984, UK

A smartly dressed woman drags a fur coat behind her, leaving a trail of blood in her wake. The blood is the only color in the image, heightening the shock effect on the viewer. Featuring photography provided for free by David Bailey, this 1980s poster, originally published by Greenpeace, went on to became one of the most iconic campaigns in the UK. Adopted by the antifur organization Lynx—a splinter group of campaigners from Greenpeace formed in 1985—the poster was accompanied by a movie ad and helped change consumer attitudes to wearing fur. The luxury department store Harrods closed its fur department in 1990, the ultimate indication of the campaign's success. The publicity garnered was equally as notable for the way it furthered the antifur cause, ushering in a new campaigning style—a combination of celebrity support and hard-hitting advertising—and flipping the focus from animal cruelty to fur-wearers as social pariahs.

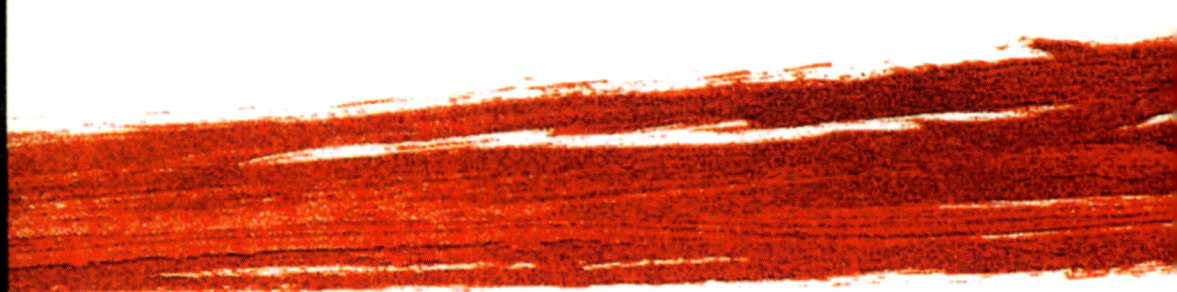

> "WHAT WE ARE DOING TO THE FORESTS OF THE WORLD IS BUT A MIRROR REFLECTION OF WHAT WE ARE DOING TO OURSELVES AND TO ONE ANOTHER . . ."
>
> *Mahatma Gandhi*
> INDIAN CIVIL RIGHTS ACTIVIST

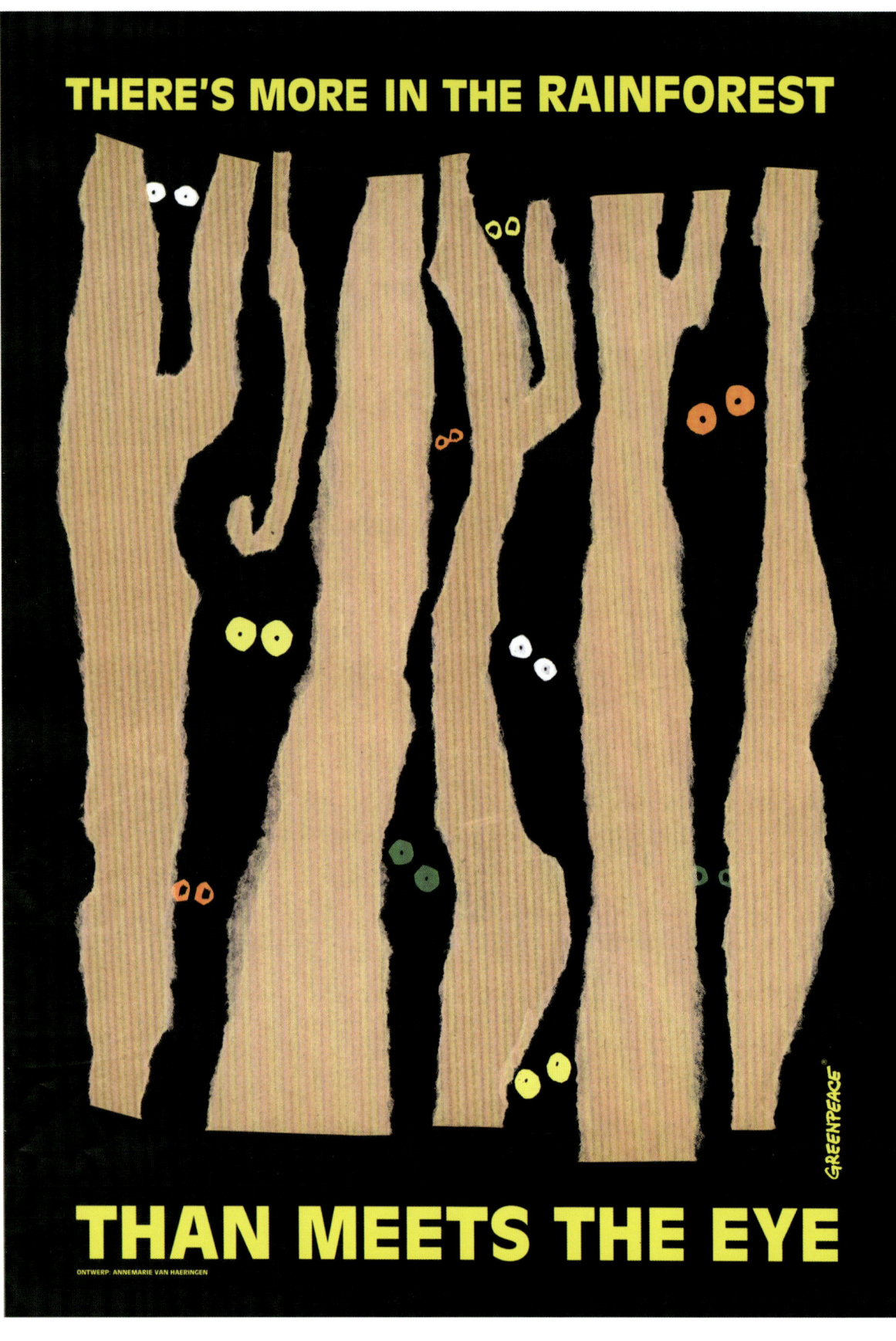

There's More In The Rainforest Than Meets The Eye
Annemarie van Haeringen for Greenpeace
c. 1980s, Netherlands

"Save the Rainforest" was a rallying cry of the 1980s and 1990s that harnessed celebrity concern as people began to grasp the global enormity of the problems that devastation of the Amazon rainforest caused. Designed by an award-winning Dutch illustrator, this poster uses the strapline "There's more in the rainforest than meets the eye" to highlight the complexities and catastrophe of deforestation. Against a matte-black background, torn strips of brown paper portray the Amazon rainforest's trees, through which there can be seen several pairs of eyes. The Amazon is home to over a million species of plants and animals—that we know of—and has been described as "the lungs of the earth." Deforestation doesn't only endanger the biodiversity; it depletes a valuable "sponge" that absorbs CO^2 emissions, a huge volume of which are released through the burning of rainforests.

Und Macht Euch Die Erde Untertan
Klaus Staeck
1987, Germany

This poster shows the earth atop a lemon squeezer underneath a slogan that reads "Und Macht Euch Die Erde Untertan" ("Subdue the Earth"). As a wry reverberation of the bible verse Genesis 1:28—"God blessed them and said to them Be fruitful and increase in number; fill the earth and subdue it. Rule over the fish in the sea and the birds in the sky and over every living creature that moves on the ground"—it is a powerful message about our misappropriation of the earth's resources, and of our abuse of power: humans literally squeeze the earth dry. It was designed by Klaus Staeck, a German lawyer better known for his political posters, who since the sixties has produced more than three hundred on social, political, and environmental issues. He collaborated often with fellow German artist and environmentalist Joseph Beuys. Staeck has been taken to court many times—forty-one to be exact—but has won every single case in a triumph for freedom of speech.

THE ART OF PROTEST 159

Superphénix . . . Débranchez-le!
Les Europeens Contre Superhénix
1994, France

The nuclear power plant Superphénix—a fast-breeder reactor and the first of its type in the world—had courted controversy since its construction was approved in 1972. Sited at Creys-Malville in France, close to the Swiss border, the prototype reactor suffered ongoing operational issues and was forced to close in 1990. In 1994, it got the go-ahead to restart for "research purposes," which many took to mean keeping foreign investors happy and the local population employed. This poster, with its call to "Unplug it!" ("Débranchez-le!"), urges people to take to the streets to protest the decision. A walk across France from Malville to Matignon in Brittany was organized by Les Europeens Contre Superphénix and covered almost nine hundred kilometers. En route was a stop that commemorated the victims of the 1986 Chernobyl disaster. Because of Superphénix's history of unreliability, the real fear of an explosion is echoed in the poster's artwork: a destroyed nuclear plant looms over two children who are playing among the debris, their colorful ball symbolic of their childhood and a beacon that further exposes the threat of nuclear power stations. Although the reactor did begin operating again, it was closed for good in 1997.

> **"WHEN THE LAST TREE IS CUT AND THE LAST FISH KILLED, THE LAST RIVER POISONED, THEN YOU WILL SEE THAT YOU CAN'T EAT MONEY."**
>
> *John May*
> COAUTHOR OF *THE GREENPEACE STORY*

International Day of Action against Dams and for Rivers, Water and Life
Roberto Arroyo
Early 2000s, pre 2007, USA

The International Day of Action for Rivers (as it is now called) takes place every year on March 14. The movement started in 1997 in Brazil, instigated by participants of the first International Meeting of People Affected by Dams. The day is both a protest against destructive water projects, such as dam-building and the harm they cause surrounding communities, and a campaign for more sustainable management of rivers. This poster was published by the International Rivers Network, who work in Latin America, Asia, and Africa to protect rivers and defend the rights of communities that depend on them. Against a green background, it shows an intertwined male and female figure. Their bodies flow into one another, as does the water coursing through them. The image reflects both solidarity with communities adversely affected by dam-building and the importance of a healthy waterway to their way of life. There is a colorful fish on the bottom right of the poster swimming in the water-circle that flows through the figures, which are encircled by the words "Water for life, not for death!" in a number of different languages.

Environmental Justice
Ricardo Levins Morales
2006, USA

This poster, from Puerto Rican-born poster artist and activist Ricardo Levins Morales, uses Hokusai's *The Great Wave* as the basis for a call for environmental justice: namely, a fair and inclusive way of dealing with environmental issues. Standing opposite the wave is a group of people. Out front a female figure holds a baby with one arm while raising the other to stop the oncoming wave and its cargo of oil drums and other pollution. The concept of environmental justice emerged as a response to the propensity of environmentalism to be elitist. The impact of environmental devastation disproportionally affects poor and indigenous communities. What's often offered up as a solution is only a displacement of the initial problem to areas of poverty, such as the siting of landfills on indigenous lands or the inequitable disposal of toxic waste.

Stop Climate Change Before It Changes You
Germaine ad agency for the World Wide Fund for Nature (WWF), known as the World Wildlife Fund in the US and Canada
2008, Europe

This image of a hybrid fish-man was the brainchild of a Belgian advertising agency that produced this European campaign for the WWF—the world's largest conservation organization. Primarily a print campaign, it was accompanied by a television commercial and public appearances of activists wearing fish-head masks, dubbed the "FishMen Guerilla campaign." The image presents the viewer with an uncomfortable truth concerning the consequences of inaction on climate change. The function of the fish persona is both a reference to rising sea levels and an extreme interpretation of mutations due to climate change, using fear to elicit action: "Stop Climate Change Before It Changes You."

Shell. Own Up. Pay Up. Clean Up.
Amnesty International
2012, UK

This poster shows Cecilia Teela, a shellfish collector, as she searches for periwinkles in the oil-polluted Bodo creek in the Niger Delta, in 2011. Three years earlier, two huge oil spills had devastated the area, destroying native ecosystems and, with it, many locals' livelihoods. To the right of Cecilia, the Shell logo is set within a smear of dripping, sticky oil above the command: "Shell. Own Up. Pay Up. Clean Up." Shell did eventually own up, although they originally blamed the spill on sabotage and downplayed the amount of oil spilled. Their initial compensation offer was paltry—the equivalent of $5,000 for the whole community—but after a claim brought against them in the UK courts on behalf of 69,000 Nigerians, they agreed to pay £55 million ($70 million US dollars). However, the pollution has never been cleaned up. The area remains devastated, with many forced to work farther afield to make a living. Food shortages and higher prices, along with dirty, polluted water, have a huge impact on local residents' health.

It's Getting Hot In Here
Mary Tremonte, Justseeds
2013, USA

Mary Tremonte—a founding member of Justseeds Artists' Cooperative—designed this poster after hearing about the plight of polar bears in the face of icebergs melting due to the global climate crisis. The International Polar Bear Agreement celebrated its fortieth anniversary in 2013. The agreement originally cited hunting and mining for oil development as the main threats to the polar bear population. Since then, the increase in sea-ice retreat poses a more serious danger, and the climate crisis is now the biggest threat to the survival of polar bears. This polar bear carries a bindle bag, and the accompanying text, "It's getting hot in here," reflects the reality that polar bears face—their habitat is literally disappearing—and underlines the critical nature of the problem.

"Killer Bags"
Surfers Against Sewage (SAS)
Plastic Free Coastlines
2014, UK

Devised by Surfers Against Sewage (SAS)—a UK-based environmental charity that grew from a small surfing community in South West England—this poster tackles the present-day plastic pollution problem. When SAS started, raw sewage waste was wrecking the oceans and beaches. Now plastic pollution is the nemesis and this image of a plastic bag fashioned as a fish is the new reality. In fact, the bag seen here was captured by photographer Martin Brent while diving in Greece. Along with two other images portraying plastic bags as sea creatures, this image was part of a series called "Killer Bags," which illustrated SAS's "Break The Bag Habit" campaign to highlight the danger plastic poses to sealife and to curb the issue of single-use bags. The campaign was launched prior to the UK's introduction in 2015 of a charge for plastic bags.

Daddy, what did YOU do in the Climate War?
Josh MacPhee, Justseeds
2017, USA

Using the same play on guilt, a reworking of a British recruitment poster from 1915—"Daddy, what did YOU do in the Great War?"—forms the basis of this poster from Josh MacPhee, a founding member of artists' collective Justseeds. It was produced for the 2017 People's Climate March, held at the end of President Trump's first one hundred days in office, to protest against his environmental policies. The father and his children are drawn wearing diving helmets as their living room fills with water—a visual allusion to the earth's rising sea levels—and the use of the word "war" enforces the gravity of climate change upon the viewer. As MacPhee explains: "My goal is to both equate the seriousness of our current climate crisis with one of the bloodiest wars humans have seen, but also playfully jab at the extremes we tend to go to in order to pretend things are 'normal.' There is no normal any more."

AFTERWORD
BY AMNESTY INTERNATIONAL

Not Here. But Now.
Walker for
Amnesty International
2006, Switzerland

This series of posters (shown opposite and on the following page) places the issue of human rights literally in front of our eyes. More than 200 posters were displayed in cities around Switzerland. Using real reportage photographs, each meticulously matched its surroundings, creating the impression that the scene in the poster was actually happening in front of passers-by.

This book is a brilliant and eclectic collection of protest art created by people seeking to change the world. The images and words speak truth to power with flair and wit. Some of it is a hundred years old—but still shines with the passion and conviction of its long-gone makers.

Human rights are not abstract concepts; they are rules rooted in shared values that reflect the best of humanity, values of equality, truth, and justice. Human rights are defined and protected by law. Those in authority are not allowed to pick and choose which rights, if any, they will respect in their pursuit of profit and power.

It took centuries of struggle and protest to achieve the precious freedoms we have today. Our international human rights laws cover all the issues featured in *The Art of Protest.* We have the right to asylum, gender and racial equality, peace, freedom of expression, healthcare, education, and a safe, clean, healthy, and sustainable environment. Huge strides in social progress have been achieved at least in part thanks to brave and persistent protesters. Those who, in Bob Marley's words, "Get up, stand up, stand up for your rights. Get up, stand up, don't give up the fight."

We must be ever-vigilant. Our rights are not set in stone: they are always susceptible to erosion. This is why the human right to peaceful protest is fundamental to a free society. It is closely bound to the right to freedom of expression, which allows writers and artists to flourish, and all of us to laugh, weep, sing, and enjoy the arts—and to be angry when these freedoms are violated.

Creative defiance and poking fun at those in charge can take courage as well as *joie de vivre*. Protest is an indomitable spark in humanity—but our right to protest is not universally favored by those in authority. In many cases it carries severe risks—protesters can be derided, arrested, imprisoned, tortured, and even face death.

Amnesty International is a global movement of millions of ordinary people standing up for humanity and human rights. We are happy to see that some of our posters have made it into this collection—they are from many countries and show how we have stood up against oppression since we were founded in 1961. We are proud to stand up for freedom, whenever and wherever it is needed. We hope this book inspires you to do the same.

www.amnesty.org.uk
www.amnestyusa.org

SOURCES

P14–33: NO HUMAN BEING IS ILLEGAL . . .
Articles, interviews, and essays
Cross, Tony: "Migration: the long, hard road from Portugal to France." *RFI*. December 13, 2018
Faux, Jeff: "How US Foreign Policy Helped Create the Immigration Crisis." *The Nation*. October 18, 2017
Gambino, Lauren: "'No human being is illegal': linguists argue against mislabeling of immigrants." *The Guardian*. December 6, 2015
Giorgis, Hannah: "The Faulty Logic in Trump's Travel Ban." *The Atlantic*. January 13, 2019
Jardine, Alexandra: "Noma Bar's Powerful Amnesty International Illustration Captures the Horror of Border Separations." *AdAge*. June 26, 2018
McNamara, Sara: "Posters, Politics and immigration during the May 1968 Protests in France." University of New Orleans Theses and Dissertations: ScholarWorks@ UNO. December 17, 2010
Nadi, Selim: "Immigrant Struggles, Anti-Racism, and May 1968: An Interview with Daniel A. Gordon." *Viewpoint Magazine*. October 5, 2017
Recinos, Eva: "The L.A. Illustrator Behind This Viral DACA Protest Art Wants More Than 'Likes'. *LA Weekly*. September 25, 2017
Tseng-Putterman, Mark: "A Century of U.S. Intervention Created the Immigration Crisis." *Medium*. June 21, 2018

Digital collections and archives
Library of Congress collections
Palestine Poster Project
Smithsonian American Art Museum collections
University of North Texas collections

Museums and other organizations
Amnesty International
anishkapoor.com
Justseeds
Maghrebins.ca
National Museum of Mexican Art
Peter Drew Arts
Ricardo Levins Morales Art Studio Online Store
The Gilder Lehrman Institute of American History
United Nations High Commissioner for Refugees (UNHCR)

P36–55: WOMEN ARE LIKE TEABAGS . . .
Articles, interviews, and essays
Crawford, Elizabeth: "Suffrage Stories/Women Artists: Caroline Watts And the 'Bugler Girl'." *Woman and Her Sphere*. December 3, 2014
Mortimer, Caroline: "How 100,000 Russian women helped create International Women's Day 100 years ago." *The Independent*. March 8, 2017
"Women Of The World, Unite! International Women's Day In Soviet-Era Posters." *Radio Free Europe, Radio Liberty Photo Gallery*. March 8, 2018

Digital collections and archives
Center for the Study of Political Graphics collections
Mondo Beat Magazine online archive
Museum of London Collections

Museums and other organizations
Amplifier
docspopuli.org (Lincoln Cushing)
Ohio History Connection
Rose O'Neill and Bonniebrook Museum
Syracuse Cultural Workers

P58–77: IF A BULLET SHOULD ENTER MY BRAIN . . .
Articles, interviews, and essays
Act-Up Paris: "Les 20 ans d'Act Up-Paris vu par l'école de l'image 'Les Gobelins'."
Clews, Colin: "1984 'Pits and Perverts' Benefit Concert." *Gayinthe8os.com*. May 27, 2013

El Khatib, Khalid: "After 27 Years, fierce pussy Is Still Making Inescapable Lesbian Art." *them*. June 6, 2018
Finkelstein, Avram: "Silence = Death: How An Iconic Protest Poster Came Into Being." *Literary Hub*. December 1, 2017
Hill, Eli: "The Lesbian Artists Who Reclaim Homophobic Slurs with Provocative Posters." *Artsy*. November 30, 2018
Kellaway, Kate: "When miners and gay activists united: the real story of the film Pride." *The Observer*. August 31, 2014

Digital collections and archives
Berkeley Library University of California. Gay Bears: The Hidden History of the Berkeley Campus
Bishopsgate Institute Special Collections and Archives
Center for the Study of Political Graphics collections
Manuscripts and Archives Division, The New York Public Library Digital Collections
Oakland Museum of California (OMCA) collections

Museums and other organizations
Amnesty International
Fondation Émergence
British Library: archive of exhibition: *Gay UK: Love, Law and Liberty at the British Library: a new exhibition marking the 50th anniversary of the Sexual Offences Act 1967*
Centers for Disease Control and Prevention (CDC)
Gay Men's Health Crisis (GMHC)
Stonewall, UK
Syracuse Cultural Workers

P80–101: THOSE WHO LOVE PEACE . . .
Articles, interviews, and essays
Austoni, Andrea: "The Legacy Of Polish Posters." *Smashing Magazine*. January 17, 2010
Ford, Tim: "The Peace Movement that Defined the Vietnam War." *Misericordia University history projects*
Heller, Steven: "War Is Not Healthy: The True Story." *American Institute of Graphic Arts (AIGA)*. September 20, 2005
Swann, Thom: David Gentleman. *Grafik.net*. February 13, 2015

Digital collections and archives
Hiroshima Peace Memorial Museum online database
Imperial War Museum collections
Museum of Modern Art (MoMA) collections
Swarthmore College Peace Collection, Vietnam Summer Records
The V&A collections

Museums and other organizations
Smithsonian American Art Museum
Quakers in Britain

104–123: UNTHINKING RESPECT FOR AUTHORITY . . .
Articles, interviews, and essays
Brammer, John Paul: "A Nonbinary Artist Made the Most Popular Poster at the March For Our Lives." *them*. March 26, 2018
DeAsis, Anita; Gali, Morning Star; Gomez, Krea; Gould Corrina: "Decolonize Oakland: Creating a More Radical Movement." *Occupy Oakland*, December 3, 2011
Haggerty, Taylor: "Forty years ago, a mob of students stormed the Bank of America building." *Daily Nexus*, University of California, Santa Barbara. February 25, 2010
Harvard Magazine Alumni: "The Fist and Its Clencher." July, 1998
Hunter, Walt: "The Story Behind the Poem on the Statue of Liberty." *The Atlantic*. January 16, 2018
Klos, Anna: "The Cuban Poster." November 9, 2017. *Retroavangarda*
Kuz, Michal: "High Noon and Polish Freedom: A History of Mutual Respect." *VoegelinView*. January 5, 2012

Lambert, Craig: "Echoes of 1969. Recalling a time of trial, and its continuing resonances." *Harvard Magazine.* March-April 2019
Lopinsky, Tiffany: *The Anti-War Protests at Harvard University, The Debate over the Takeover of University Hall* (Film). 2011
McKernan, Bethan: "The Kurdish woman building a feminist democracy and fighting Isis at the same time." *The Independent.* January 5, 2017
Meltzer, Erica: "LOOK: 'Is Colorado in America?'" *Denverite.* February 2, 2017
Popeson, Pamela: "New Polish Posters." *Inside/Out*, MoMA. October 15, 2010
Scherr, Judith: "Wall Street protests come to Berkeley." *Berkeleyside.* October 9, 2011
Stokoe, Claire: "51 Powerful Propaganda Posters And The People Behind." *Smashing Magazine.* June 13, 2010
Szalavitz, Maia: "Study: 1 in 3 Americans Arrested By Age 23." *time.com.* December 19, 2011

Books and journals
Bonnell, Victoria E. *Iconography of Power: Soviet Political Posters under Lenin and Stalin.* University of California Press; New Ed edition (29 Sept. 1999) pp.21-37

Digital collections and archives
British Library collections
David Pollack Vintage Posters
Library of Congress collections
Ospaaal.com
Political Posters, Labadie Collection, University of Michigan
Ulster University, CAIN web service

Museums and other organizations
Amnesty International
Die Föderation deutschsprachiger Anarchist*innen (FdA)
France 3 Hauts-de-France
Justseeds
Slingshot Collective

P126–145: HATE IS TOO GREAT A BURDEN . . .
Articles, interviews, and essays
Budds, Diana: "Black Lives Matter, The Brand." *Fast Company.* September 14, 2016
Crosfield, Hugh: "A Visual Introduction to Boycott Outspan Action and the Blood-Citrus Topos." *Chomping at the Bloodied Bit*
Davis, Jennifer: "Squeezing Apartheid." *Bulletin of Atomic Scientists.* November, 1993
Garza, Alicia: "A Herstory of the #BlackLivesMatter Movement." *the feministwire.* October 7, 2014
Gumede, William: "Mandela death: How a prisoner became a legend." *BBC Magazine.* December 7, 2013
Hain, Peter: "How apartheid poisoned the world." *The Spectator.* December 15, 2018
Marks, Ben: "Trailing Angela Davis, from FBI Flyers to 'Radical Chic' Art." *Collectors Weekly.* January 22, 2015
Petitjean, Olivier (translation): "Remembering French Investments in Apartheid South Africa." *Multinationals Observatory.* December 17, 2013
Southall, Nick: "Obituary: Michael Callaghan: Artist – Raconteur – Reader – Collector – Pleasure Seeker – Holder of Hearts." *Revolts Now.* May 7, 2013
Wicker, Tom: "Investing in Apartheid." *The New York Times.* December 6, 1977

Books and journals
MCA Collection, Volume 1, Museum of Contemporary Art (Sydney, N.S.W.)
Nerys, John: *The Campaign against British Bank Involvement in Apartheid South Africa, African Affairs*, Vol. 99, No. 396 (OUP. Jul., 2000), pp. 415-433

Digital collections and archives
African Activist Archive
Alabama Department of Archives and History Digital Collections
BlackPast
The Freedom Archives
Shwano City-County Library Digital Collections, Wisconsin Historical Society

Museums and other organizations
Black Lives Matter
Casula Powerhouse Arts Centre
dhorubabinwahad.com
docspopuli.org (Lincoln Cushing)
Forward to Freedom: The History of the British Anti-Apartheid Movement 1959-1994
The Gilder Lehrman Institute of American History
historygraphicdesign.com
Idle No More
Justseeds
Ken Sprague Fund
Milwaukee Public Museum, Indian Country Wisconsin
Museum of Contemporary Art, Australia
Museum of Modern Art (MoMA)
National Civil Rights Museum
National Gallery of Victoria, Melbourne
Smithsonian American Art Museum
South African History Online

148–168: WE ARE USING RESOURCES . . .
Articles, interviews, and essays
Grant, Sheena: How Lynx set the fur flying, January 23, 2012, *East Anglian Daily Times*
Macleod, Duncan: WWF FishMen in Belgium, December 17, 2009: *theinspirationroom.com*
Nuclear Monitor, issue #409, April 1994, *Wise International*
Rossman, Michael: The Evolution of the Social Serigraphy Movement In the San Francisco Bay Area, 1966-1986 (catalogue-essay for the exhibition *Speak! You Have the Tools!* at the de Saisset Museum of Santa Clara University, 1987. Republished as web essay, 2007: Michael Rossman, *Writings and Then Some*)

Books and journals
Epstein, Barbara: *Political Protest and Cultural Revolution: Nonviolent Direct Action in the 1970s and 1980s.*University of California Press; New Ed edition (3 Sept. 1993) pp80-91
Surbrug, Robert: *Beyond Vietnam: The Politics of Protest in Massachusetts, 1974-1990.* University of Massachusetts Press; Culture, Politics, and Cold War series edition (September 29, 2009) pp77-98

Digital collections and archives
International Institute of Social History (Amsterdam)
Memory of the Netherlands
The National Museum of American History collections
The Advertising Archives

Museums and other organizations
Amnesty International
Anarchy in Action
California State University, Northridge
docspopuli.org (Lincoln Cushing)
Earth Day Network
International Rivers
Justseeds
Library of Congress
National Park Service
Robert Rauschenberg Foundation
Ricardo Levins Morales Art Studio Online Store
Surfers Against Sewage
US Fish & Wildlife Service
World Wide Fund for Nature (WWF)

ACKNOWLEDGMENTS

With profound thanks to Amnesty International; in particular to Nicky Parker and Maggie Paterson, who agreed to support this ambitious project from the beginning; to Lucy Macnamara for her help coordinating the foreword; and to Clare Bullen for her time in helping to source the Amnesty posters included in this book. Thanks also to all the artists who contributed their work, but especially to Lincoln Cushing whose knowledge and dedication to documenting dissent was invaluable, and to Josh MacPhee for his generosity. Kate Dioufas, Caterina Favaretto, Aoi Matsushima, and Lotta Wolgers Gray, for assistance with translations—thank-you! And of course to Anish Kapoor for his inspiring words.

This book is for my family.

PICTURE CREDITS
B: Bottom, **L**: Left, **R**: Right, **T**: Top
Advertising Archives P163 **Alamy** P14 Chronicle, P15 Stocktrek Images, Inc., P16, P47, P83, P84 Granger Historical Picture Archive, P36, P156-157 Pictorial Press Ltd, P40, P42 The Protected Art Archive, P44 Heritage Image Partnership Ltd, P49 MARKA, P91, P94, P138 World History Archive, P99 Mark Phillips, P119 mpworks, P128B Christopher, P132 Contraband Collection **Amnesty International** P8 © Seymour Chwast, P11© Joop Lieverst , P22 © Howard Davies / Panos Pictures, P24, P51, P55, P74, P76, P118, P164 Amnesty International, P27 © Amnesty International / illustration: Pete Reynolds, P31 AIUSA, P33 Courtesy Boys + Girls © Amnesty International / illustration: Noma Bar, P116 @ Alain Carrier with the agreement of the Association des Amis d'Alain Carrier, P141 © Michael Callaghan / Amnesty Australia, P170, P172-173 Walker Agency for Amnesty Switzerland **Amplifier** P54 © Victoria García for Amplifier 2017, **Micah Bazant** P123 © Micah Bazant for Amplifier, 2018 **Bridgeman Images** P17, P130R Gilder Lehrman Collection, New York, USA, P19, P106, P153 © ADAGP, Paris and DACS, London 2019, P25, P121 Pictures from History, P43 French School, (20th century) / Bibliotheque Marguerite Durand, Paris, France / Archives Charmet, P45 French School, (20th century) / Private Collection / © Gerald Bloncourt, P46 French School, (20th century) / Private Collection / Archives Charmet, P64 American School, (20th century) / Brooklyn Museum of Art, New York, USA / Gift of Robert Thill in honor of Robin Renée Thill Beck, P71 Collection Jean Jacques Allev, P85, P131 Private Collection / Peter Newark American Pictures, P100-101 Gentleman, David (b.1930) / National Army Museum, London, P115 Bridgeman Images, P117 CGT Poster / © Gerald Bloncourt, P129 Cieciorka, Frank (1939-2008) / Private Collection, P136 French School, (20th century) / Private Collection, P148 Deutsches Historisches Museum, Berlin, Germany / © DHM, P155, P161 American School, (20th century) / Private Collection, P160 Collection Jean Jacques Allevi **British Library** P62 © Kevin Franklin, P68 © Peter Tatchell **Center for the Study of Political Graphics** P48, P50, P59, P61, P66, P111 Courtesy of Center for the Study of Political Graphics, P60, P87, P88, P98, P109, P139, P142, P152 Courtesy Lincoln Cushing / Docs Populi **Design Action Collective** P145 Courtesy of Black Lives Matter © **Peter Drew** P26 © **Jillian Edelstein** P10 **Fondation Émergence** P77 **Getty Images** P18 API/Gamma-Rapho, P41, P105 Photo by Fine Art Images/Heritage Images, P80-81 Photo by DeAgostini, P82 Michael Nicholson/Corbis via Getty Images, P86, P90, P92, P93, P96, P97 Universal History Archive/UIG via Getty Images, P95 Photo by © Historical Picture Archive/CORBIS/Corbis via Getty Images, P107, P127, P134-135 Photo by David Pollack/Corbis via Getty Images, P108 Fotosearch / Stringer, P133 Photo by MPI **The Gilder Lehrman Institute of American History** P130L, GLC06124 **International Institute of Social History** P158 © Annemarie van Haeringen, P159 © Klaus Staeck **Justseeds** P28-29, P122, P143, P168 © Josh MacPhee P144 © Jesse Purcell, P165 © Mary Tremonte © **Anish Kapoor** P30 **Ken Sprague Foundation** P126 The Ken Sprague Fund and Artery Publications, publishers of Ken Sprague - People's Artist © **Alain Le Quernec** P114 **Library of Congress** P112-113, P149 © **Ashley Lukashevsky** P32 **Memac Ogilvy & Mather Dubai for UN** P53 © **Ricardo Levins Morales** P23 (2007) P162 (2006) **National Gallery Victoria** P140 © Marie McMahon/Copyright Agency. Licensed by DACS 2019 **National Museum of American History** P150 Carl F. Meyers, Jr. Courtesy National Museum of American History, P154 Division of Political History, Archives Center, National Museum of American History, Smithsonian Institution **National Museum of Mexican Art** P20 photo: Michael Tropea **The New York Public Library** P58 Manuscripts and Archives Division, The New York Public Library **Political Posters, Labadie Collection, University of Michigan** P104 University of Michigan Library Digital Collections, **Private Collection** P137 **Rex Shutterstock** P37, P38-39 Museum of London, P70 Keystone/Zuma, P89 Granger, P110 Kharbine-Tapabor **Robert Rauschenberg Foundation** P151 © Robert Rauschenberg Foundation/VAGA at ARS, NY and DACS, London 2019 **Slingshot Media** P120 **Stonewall (UK)** P69, P72-73 **Surfers Against Sewage** P166-167 **Syracuse Cultural Workers** P52 Favianna Rodriguez and SyracuseCulturalWorkers.com, P63, P65 SyracuseCulturalWorkers.com, P67 illustration by Harry Freeman-Jones, poster by SyracuseCulturalWorkers.com © **Rommy Torrico** P75 Collaboration with TransLatin@ Coalition and Rommy Torrico, www.rommytorrico.com **United Nations High Commissioner for Refugees** P21 Courtesy Lego Group

The publishers and author have endeavored to obtain the necessary permissions to reproduce all images. Should any have been overlooked we would be grateful for further information.